Shout It From the Rooftops
Powerful Stories That Transform Lives

AUTHORS

Ruth Amanda

Kathryn Baskette

Hollis Citron

Ellen M. Craine

Sarah DeGeorge

Susan DeGeorge

Adrianne Fekete

Amy Garelick

Kelly Geisler

Daneika Glenn

Darcey Kesner Hawkins

Falyn Morningstar

Muhnoo Sophia Jain

Suzy Roundy-Schmidt

Trisha Singeltary

CREDITS

**Copyright © 2023 by
I Am Creative Publishing**

All rights reserved. Apart from any fair dealing for the purpose of research or private study, or criticism or review, as permitted under the Copyright, Designs and Patents Act 1988, this publication may only be reproduced, stored or transmitted, in any form or by any means, with the prior permission in writing of the copyright owner, or in the case of the reprographic reproduction in accordance with the terms of licensees issued by the Copyright Licensing Agency. Enquiries concerning reproduction outside those terms should be sent to the publisher.

ISBN: 979-8-9891367-2-8

DEDICATION

A heartfelt thank you for all of you that are reading this and are open to various perspectives. We learn and grow with all of the moments we have if we are willing to be present and not be judgmental.

Thank you to all of my contributors that said **Yes** and have been vulnerable to share a part of themselves. You are incredible humans and I am so grateful to know you.

Thank you to my illustrator Sophie Lane for having the vision to bring this book to life by creating this cover that is so colorful and vibrant.

This is my **shout it** for all to hear and take it as you wish.

" Overthinking is not creative thinking" –Hollis Citron

Sending so much love your way.

CONTENT

Introduction

You'll Be OK	1
Ruth Amanda	12
Being Peaceful is Having a Warrior's Soul	14
Kathryn Baskette	17
I Didn't Love Every Job I Had	19
Hollis Citron	23
It's Hard to Care for an Aging Parent	25
Ellen Craine	34
It's Okay to Say "No"	36
Sarah DeGeorge	48
It's Never Too Late To Follow Your Dreams!	49
	59
Susan DeGeorge	
Embracing Growth and Freedom	60
Adrianne Fekete	64
It's Okay to Ask for Help	66
Amy Garelick	69
Your Extraordinary Life is Waiting for You!	71
Kelly Geisler	84

You Are Here to Live By Your Own Lights	86
Daneika Glenn	101
Born to Break the Shame	103
Darcey Kesner Hawkins	117
Pleasure and Vitality are Your Birthright	119
Falyn Morningstar	135
Embrace yourself! Be kind to yourself!	137
Muhnoo Sophia Jain	140
Showing Up Messy	142
Suzy Roundy-Schmidt	148
People Can Change	150
Trisha Singeltary	153
I Am Creative Publishing	155

INTRODUCTION

This collection of stories is all about that moment when you want to climb up the mountain, grab your megaphone and just Shout It From The Rooftops what you have learned along this life journey. You get to look into the lens of these incredible women's worlds, and see how much you can benefit from their wisdom.

Each and every person sees life through their lens. We may go through similar experiences BUT not have the same takeaways. These individuals that raised their hand to share their stories realized that they have something to say and it is worthy of being heard.

Sharing with each other forms stronger connections as individuals and as a society. Through storytelling we do not feel so isolated in our experiences and can feel seen, while also being open to the perspective of learning something new.

These powerful stories range from overcoming physical and emotional imbalances in a holistic way to not holding back any more and following one's dreams. In the fluctuations of life's circumstances there are dark times, quiet and still times that could be perceived as boring and the other extreme of happy and joyful times. The beauty of it all is in truly owning our personal transformation, as Kelly Geisler says in her chapter. We are all works in progress and truly have the potential to have an extraordinary life.

There is something in here for everyone to have as a takeaway. This may be a rainbow and unicorn statement but these multi author spaces are a platform to have the ability to change the world. Multiple people can share their viewpoint on a particular topic in one space. By taking the time to listen to one another, truly listen and see and accept each other for who we are and not who we want them to be, the possibilities are endless.

As you read along, visualize what is your Shout It From The Rooftops? What is your Powerful Story That Transforms Lives? Speak it out loud and share it with others. The ripple effect is strong!

YOU'LL BE OK

But I Don't Want to Spoil the Ending

Ruth Amanda

S everal years back, my mother had a stroke. As a child, mom had a heart murmur and a bout of rheumatic fever, but she grew up to be a pretty sturdy lady, with strong convictions and a strength of will few can match. There was an open-heart surgery around the time that I was born (the second of four children) but it was barely a pause in her determined stride. She was creative, persistent, and strong. In my teen years, Mom realized her own happiness by purchasing a farm and set about raising beef cattle. While in her seventies, she continued running the farm with a vitality which had left no clue of the impending stroke.

Doctors put her on a priority list for surgery, but sent her home with a regimen of pills for varying issues. I still recall with laughter Mom grumbling about the blood thinners being rat poison. Were they trying to cure her, or kill her? There were also instructions about suitable activities, amongst which mingling with her cattle was considered a no-no. The sacrilege! Did the doctors know she was a farmer? How do you farm without being with the cows?

When the surgery finally happened, it was long and hard. She spent weeks in ICU, heavily sedated. During this time, I found a "SIGN" (a.k.a. a plaque) in the hospital gift shop. "Not to spoil the ending, but everything is going to be okay…". While I found it hard to believe at the time, it made me smile and I purchased it and set it on the rolling hospital tray across the foot of Mom's bed where she might see it when she came out of sedation.

Mom awoke very feisty (an adjective meaning "cross", "perturbed", "more than vaguely annoyed"). It was a justifiable attitude and can be an asset when you're needing to heal. She seemed annoyed by the plaque, saying "Of course it will be okay! How maudlin!" When I offered to move the plaque, she insisted it be put back where it was.

She recovered fully and went on to have many more years of wonderful crotchety-ness mixed with sarcasm and giggles. Our relationship had always been difficult, but as she recovered so did our relationship, through Life's many ups and downs in those next few years.

THE GIFT THAT KEPT ON GIVING
Over the coming months, I would get frustrated about something and the "SIGN" would show up in my mailbox. Mom might have a setback, and I'd drive up to my parents' home, leaving the "SIGN" where Mom might find it, like her sock drawer, or her potting shed. The "SIGN" kept passing on its words of wisdom, time after time.

"Not to spoil the ending, but everything is going to be okay…"

Prior to the stroke, there had been a period of no communication with my mom due to disagreements around some of my life choices. Having mom back in my life was wonderful. We were closer now than we had ever been before and she worked harder at understanding me.

THEN CAME CHINA

My then partner's mother wanted to go to China, but not alone, so I agreed to go with her. I was in charge of finding the itinerary we would use. I had watched "The Karate Kid" with Jackie Chan and Jayden Smith. One of the filming locations had caught my eye, and a google search revealed it to be Wudang Mountain. I was determined to fit it into the itinerary. I asked the travel agent if it could be an add-on to the end of our trip. She looked into it, and removed another stop from the plan, and inserted Wudang Mountain into that space. I was ready to go!

I packed my bags, took a photo of the "SIGN" with my phone so I would have it nearby when the trip became frustrating (as it surely would, personality differences being what they are) and set off for the airport. I looked at the "SIGN" often during that trip, but also luxuriated in the history around me. The beauty of the art and culture, the magnificence of the feats of engineering, the stories of China's heroes and villains, and the magnificent food offerings, did not disappoint. I was alive with anticipation as our trip brought us down the Yangtze to debark and travel cross country by car to Wudang Mountain.

THE MOUNTAIN

Wudang Mountain has been a center of religious activities since before 770 BC. It is the number one Taoist mountain in China and is the birthplace of Tai Chi (and Kung Fu depending on who you ask). Chinese Taoism puts emphasis on a harmonious combination of Taoism, Confucianism and Buddhism. Now designated a UNESCO World Heritage site, its flanks are dotted with temples, monasteries, bridges and shrines. Its peaks reach to heaven. It's also a great place to improve your cardio--the mountain is crisscrossed with trails and thousands of stairs!

The deep red walls of buildings, and their green tiled rooftops, rise from her slopes. Gold leaf, brightly painted pillars and frescoes adorn their facades. Taoist monks mingle with martial artists. The deep tones of gongs resonate through the air. Red prayer ribbons waft in the breeze from every tree and railing like streamers of hope for what could be. I knew I was meant to come here.

Traditionally, pilgrims to this mountain start at the bottom of the mountain before dawn. They would hike the steep slopes and stairways, crossing bridges of rock and stone, pausing to pray at various shrines along the way. They might make offerings or beg hospitality at one of the many monasteries along the way. Their goal, the Golden Summit.

Eric, my guide, assisted me in purchasing some red prayer ribbons and some joss sticks and I slid them into my daypack. My journey started after breakfast, with the sun already risen. First we went by Eco bus to a certain stopping point below the main peak, and then by cable car to a spot not far from the Golden Summit. From the bus, I could see glimpses of people climbing the ancient trail in the traditional way. When we disembarked to catch the cable car, there was a small plaza full of shops, and business was clearly booming here. I shrugged it off and got in the cable car.

My ears popped a couple of times before we reached the top of the cables and I knew my own pilgrimage was beginning. Thankfully, my travel companion opted to sit at a tea house and admire scenery instead of "doing all that superstitious stuff" so I was freed to enjoy it properly. My research and Eric had both told me that there were many small temples and shrines between here and the Golden Summit. We would be starting at the Hall of Luck. As I climbed the stairs in the thin air at this elevation, I was praying already. Mostly for oxygen!

THE HALL OF LUCK

There was a short queue at the Hall of Luck, so Eric talked while we waited. He indicated that I should enter right leg first over the door sill. Then follow his lead to perform the "ritual" for this hall which would end with the monk inside ringing a small gong, when we could exit--but I should not touch the door frame or sill when departing, or the luck would brush off. I smiled at the sternness with which he gave these instructions, but was careful stepping into the dark, musty interior of the hall. In the dim light of candles, I could make out a tiny monk sitting on a cushion in the corner next to a low table and a gong. Eric knelt on a cushion before a Buddha and kowtowed, forehead to the floor, then rose and stepped back. I did the same, sending out my prayer that luck would follow me on this journey. Then we inched into a gap between the wall and the shrine and very slowly shuffled through this narrow gap all the way around it. I added an extra prayer that no spiders were hiding in the space as I shuffled along. Emerging from the other side of the shrine, the candlelight seemed brighter after the tight darkness of the passage as we emerged. Kowtowing once more, I held my forehead to the ground until the small gong was struck. Thwooongg!

Rising, I bowed slightly to the monk in the corner, and then turned to leave. I paused to allow another monk to enter before carefully leaving the hall without touching the doorframe or sill. Right leg first.

Smiling at my guide in the sunshine, I brushed some dirt from my jeans and asked where to next.

THE MONK

A voice spoke from behind me in rapid Chinese, causing Eric to smile and bow. I turned, and the monk from the Hall of Luck was there. Eric indicated that the monk had a question for me, if I wouldn't mind using him as interpreter. I smiled and agreed and the following conversation ensued.

"What brings you to the Mountain?"
"I came for the history and…"
"No, he wants to know why you really came to the Mountain."
"Oh, I guess I wanted to learn something but I don't know what that is. I just know I felt pulled to come here so I made it happen."
"And the joss sticks in your pack?"
"For the temples. I want to follow the traditions you use here."

A nod and smile from the monk, then, "You will pass many halls and temples. Your guide will tell you about them and he will help you. Follow his instructions. If you open your heart and your mind, and truly wish to learn, the mountain will teach you. Do you believe there is a higher power? A God?"

I nodded, so he added, "On the Mountain it does not matter what you call that power. You may call it God or Allah or any other name. It only matters that you acknowledge that power which surrounds us. If you send your thoughts and prayers out, the answers will come back to you. It doesn't matter if you kneel or kowtow or bow to the East when you pray. It only matters that you pray."

He began to turn away, so I bowed slightly again, receiving one in return. As he shuffled off, Eric and I resumed our path.

THE CLIMB
My guide told me that we better follow the monk's instructions to be respectful, so we should next stop at the Hall of Parents.

I followed him down a path, up some stairs, and into the Hall of Parents. On the way, Eric explained that this hall had many purposes. A couple might pray to conceive a child, or pray for their parents. Withdrawing a joss stick from my pack, I lit it, held it with overlapping hands in front of my chest and took a deep breath. Bowing carefully, I let my thoughts flow toward my mother and her upcoming heart surgery and some complications she had to deal with. I set the sticks in the sand filled cauldron before the altar, letting the sweet-scented smoke waft over me. I let it go. I felt calm seeping in to fill its place.

Further down the path, up more stairs, we reached the Hall of Children. A parent might pray that a child be healthy or successful, or, again, to conceive. Final exams were approaching for my sons. Another joss stick was taken out, and as I bowed, my thoughts flowed toward their success. My thoughts flowed toward the youngest that his health would continue to be strong after some childhood setbacks. I prayed all three would become men I could admire. I was already inordinately proud of them. Again, I felt an increased sense of calm fill the gaps left by the outward flow of thoughts.

Climbing ever higher on the mountain, I continued praying. I tied ribbons on trees, with thoughts for a successful job hunt and for my own continued good health. A silly prayer for a dog accompanied another ribbon onto a branch, as I was missing that bond, having no pets at the time.

A couple of times I asked my guide, "How many more stairs?"
His inevitable reply, "Not so many, maybe 150…" and then he laughed when he heard me mutter about Chinese misinterpretation of English numbers. Onward we would go.

The Hall of War, my guide explained, was now more of a Hall of Business Success, and so I prayed for success with an investment I had made. Other halls came and went along the path. At each stop, short of breath, I discovered I wasn't just feeling light-headed, but I felt my feet and my heart grow lighter also. I felt rejuvenated. I centered my thoughts on what my prayers should be next.

As I reached the top of a flight of steps, I lifted my head and gasped.

Gleaming bright among misty clouds, we had reached the Golden Summit. A small, dark wooden pavilion with a gap of gold.

THE GOLDEN SUMMIT

My guide smiled, "You've made it!"

I asked, "And now?"

He shrugged, "Whatever is left." He turned toward the shrine, and began to kowtow three times.

I thought back over everything I had prayed about up to this point. Images of the people I loved passed through my mind. As a tear rolled down my cheek, I knelt beside my guide and kowtowed three times to the shrine, as seemed appropriate. When I rose, I pulled one last prayer ribbon from my pack and tied it to the railing around the plateau and quietly whispered, "Thank you!"

As I turned, I glanced around the summit. Some pilgrims had prayer rugs and were face downward to the East. Some were kneeling quietly, holding each other or hands raised to the heavens. No matter their posture, they all shared a common expression. Peace.

I turned back toward the stairs, but Eric caught my arm. "In Taoism, we never go backwards. Always we go forwards," he said, and led me around the shrine to a different path.

GOING FORWARD

As we descended from the peak along this new path, Eric said it would loop around to the cable car, often crossing the path we had come up. He pointed to a dirt path off to one side and told me that if we had done the old way of walking all the way up the Mountain, that path would be the traditional exit route.

As we approached that part of the Mountain where the Hall of Luck stood, we met the monk from earlier.
"Please, tell me what you learned?" he asked.
I looked up to where the Golden Summit just peeked out between green roofs and trees. I smiled. As I turned to face the monk, looking into his ancient eyes, a "SIGN" flashed through my mind. Its words were very fitting. I smiled. "I found everything is going to be okay. I found 'thank you'."

The monk took my hands in his, smiled a toothless smile, and said, "You have learned the lesson of the Mountain. The Mountain will welcome you back again."

As I continued toward the cable car, I smiled. I would be okay. Everything would be okay.

HOME AGAIN
Back home, I told Mom of my experience. As a Christian, she disagreed with some of it, but could understand the parts about prayer providing peace and was happy for me to have found some.

I think I had already made the decision to leave my partner but it took another five years to make it happen. It was a big step and took me up to Canada's Arctic with a "SIGN" wrapped carefully in tissue with a card attached, hidden in my luggage by my Mom. I hung the sign beside the bathroom mirror. I read it every morning when I woke up, and last thing at night before bed. It kept me going through two and half years of isolation from family and friends. I made new friends, discovered new adventures, and met myself again. I read, painted, laughed and discovered the me that had been pushed down by years of mental and emotional neglect.

When the time was right, the powers that be answered a prayer and I met my current husband, a man who loves and supports me no matter how weird he thinks I am at the time. I moved back to civilization and started my last fresh start…

NOT TO SPOIL THE ENDING…
I try now to consciously live each day in gratitude for what I have, in peace that things will work out as they should, and in joy for the little gifts each day. A gecko on the wall. A vibrant blossom opening in the sunshine. The sound of waves lapping on a sunlit beach.

I returned the "SIGN" to Mom when she received her cancer diagnosis and ended up in a care home alongside Dad who was now suffering from dementia. She fought the events life threw at her until she passed in 2021. Dad soldiered on, finally letting go in 2022 and being laid to rest next to her.

When David and I made a decision to downsize and move in 2022, we sorted through the bits of our memories deciding to sell, donate, or pack each one. I added the "SIGN" to the donations pile. I don't know where it ended up but I hope it reached someone who needed to hear that "Not to spoil the ending, but everything is going to be okay."

RUTH AMANDA

Life's journeys often take us down roads that feel less travelled--through valleys, over mountains, and sometimes rough weather. Ruth Amanda has been there--and hit more than a few potholes along the way! What she has learned through sharing her story with others, is that others have hit those same potholes. So many people have been to those desolate valleys and climbed out of them to reach the peaks! You are not alone.

An award winning author and illustrator, Ruth is the creator of the award-winning Geckos in the Garden, as well as There's a Buzzard on the Balcony, and There's a Seagull on my Sailboat.

Ruth Amanda is a mother (or is mother adjacent) to five grown men, and Nana to one amazing granddaughter (so far). She currently resides in Barbados with her husband David and is living her best life.

Website: www.ruthamanda.com

It's a sign

BEING PEACEFUL IS HAVING A WARRIOR'S SOUL
With Practice and Consistency We Can All Be A Peaceful Soul

Kathryn Baskette

"A Peaceful Soul"

A peaceful soul
Feels Airy
And light.
No room
For Fear
Fight or flight.

A peaceful soul
Feels free
And mighty.
A powerful strength
Aligned with
Almighty.

A peaceful soul
Means more
Than calm.
A peaceful soul
Is a power
Standing strong.

The storms
Surely come
With winds
Blowing.
Stand firm
In peace
And knowing.

There is no
Good or bad,
Only growth.
So when
You're drowning
Choose to float.

When the wind
Starts blowing
You wildly,
A peaceful soul
Will take it
Mildly.
No longer

Afraid
And frozen.
At peace
With energy
Chosen.

Earth is a school.
So, take joy
As you grow.
A peaceful soul
Will allow things
To flow.

Peace has been my soul's desire since divorce. I have practiced and meditated and prayed. I have diligently worked on not letting the chaos around me pierce through my heart and mind. It's a reminder that the war is really within ourselves and not the others who strive to hurt and destroy us. Our shield is peace no matter what. With peace, our enemies have no weapons because they cannot move us.

KATHRYN BASKETTE

K aty Baskette was born in a tiny dot of a town of south central Virginia. She has been an author since she could form words.

Her passion is poetry which is her way of connecting with God. It also serves as an outlet, a therapy to sort out and rid herself of life's pains and struggles.

The poem Katy wrote, "A Peaceful Soul," was written when journaling one day. She asked herself, "What would being peaceful feel like? What was the meaning of peaceful to her?"

The results were a powerful poem she felt she had to share.

Today, she has continued healing and wishes to serve others that have gone through similar situations. She has found peace and gratitude daily even on the harder days. Her goal is to write more poetry and stories to publish.

Facebook page: The Writings Of Katy:
https://www.facebook.com/profile.php?id=100063900500698

I DIDN'T LOVE EVERY JOB I HAD
But Each One Taught Me Skills That Were So Helpful

Hollis Citron

J obs give us the incentive to show up for the money. Spending Saturday nights babysitting was not always a first choice but being paid in cash was a bonus. Going into a mall, working in the junior department with artificial light (which always made me tired) and the same playlist was not my end all be all. Though in hindsight it all is truly a gift. Each and every one of these jobs got me to where I am today. Giving me the skills to really show up and live my passion in a way that I never knew was possible.

- The first job at around twelve years old started with the proverbial teenage job of babysitting. I learned how to always be patient, have better communication skills with parents, and kids, obviously. When the kid(s) want to play you need to play. It is not about YOU. Definitely a good form of birth control. Seeing kids have tantrums and have to change diapers at a young age made me happy to go home and not have to deal with that on the regular. When you speak clearly it gains trust with the parents. Looking back on all of that now being a parent it is a lot of trust to leave your child with a teenager, geesh.

- Then, the good old restaurant job of busing tables. I did not want the job of waitressing and did not feel I would be good at the pressure of the order. The responsibility of cleaning the table to prepare for the next sitting you needed to be fast to keep up, know how to stack the plates so they would stay balanced, collect the silverware and collect the cups and make sure they did not break and fall on the floor. To this day I still stack the plates and make sure to wipe the table down before leaving a restaurant, it is ingrained.

- Sales associate at clothing stores. So much patience !!! First off people are slobs on sales days. No respect for the space and you wanna talk about the dressing rooms. Not putting the clothes back on the hangers and just throwing them on the floor, what????? This space is all about listening to people and helping them to feel good about themselves in what they are wearing and or help them pick something out for another person. Also a big thing was having to sell credit cards. Back then they would give us incentives like earning stars and bonuses and I realized that never made me work harder. Always empathized with the customer and if they said no to a credit card, no means no.

- Art Teacher for children and adults. This job started at age 19 and is still going, thirty plus years. Creativity opens you up to be so vulnerable. Some people are open to that and others are very resistant. Everyone has a story and you do not know what is going on in anyone's world. I really learned to pay attention and read the signs of the group. Not every lesson is a winner and it took time for me to understand that it is not personal. When steps are broken down so a person can take baby steps it is less overwhelming and they can feel more successful and often surprise themself to see how capable they are and often never knew it.

- Book Publisher: All about creating safe space for people to feel expressive. My philosophy is that you do not have to know how to write to be in a book. That does not mean write a bunch of bad books. It means that everyone has a story and it needs to be shared.

The key takeaways are:
1. Patience
2. Laughter
3. Compromise
4. Say thank you
5. Acknowledge others and give compliments.
6. Don't talk so much, listen.
7. Just because you think it is a good project does not mean that others think the same thing.
8. If you drop plates in the middle of a restaurant and the whole restaurant looks at you, it happens. Builds character.
9. I am not a 9-5 kind of person. It is good to know how you function to be the most productive and dare I say happy.

10. Be flexible and open to change. If we are too structured it limits possibilities.

HOLLIS CITRON

H ollis, the Creativity Doula, guides entrepreneurs to birth their stories and get them out into the world. She is a book publisher on a mission to create spaces that give men and women permission to unleash their voice, break through blocks and confidently share their experiences and perspectives with the world. She is passionate about helping people build the confidence to recognize, encourage, and express the innate creativity that they are born with.

Creativity goes beyond the pencil and the brush. Creativity is your unique and original exploration, expansion, expression of your imagination.

Website: www.iamcreativephilly.com

Facebook: www.facebook.com/iamcreativephilly

Instagram: iamcreativephilly

Podcast that is all about connecting, inspiring and sharing stories: creativeconversations.podbean.com

IT'S HARD TO CARE FOR AN AGING PARENT
Don't Be Afraid to Ask for Help

Ellen Craine

In our society, very little discussion takes place around the challenges of caring for an aging parent. According to the National Institute on Aging, millions of Americans find themselves in the position of being a family caregiver of an older adult. (www.nia.nih.gov/health/caregiving) There is a lack of support in providing appropriate coping and navigation tools. As a social worker, and a caregiver for my eighty-six-year-old father, I want to SHOUT what I have come to understand in the hopes that it helps at least one other person/family not struggle the way my family has and is. One thing I have learned, though, is that it is important to not be afraid to ask for help. That help can come from a large number of sources and tools.

I am a caregiver with my two sisters, for our father. We are fortunate that we are able to provide 24/7 care for our father in his home. I understand that this is a luxury and recognize that most people are the actual caregivers for their aging parent on their own or with limited support or that their aging parent is in an out of home placement. Even with the luxury we have, there are multiple issues that I did not fully see coming. With these issues, I have had to empower myself to set boundaries; make sure I am taking care of myself and my two sons; all while making sure that our dad is getting the best care for the best quality of life regardless of how long in this life he has left.

Our father has moderate dementia where he is forgetful, has episodes of paranoia, and other symptoms but, gratefully, at this time, he still knows who we are. He is somewhat mobile and somewhat able to share his thoughts and feelings even if they do not always sound "logical" to us. He has a history of cancer, but there is no current diagnosis of cancer with the most recent episode being successfully treated through surgical removal in January 2023. In May, 2023, our father had a heart attack and stroke. After two days, the doctor discharged him home to die because he was having trouble swallowing. He was clear that he wanted to go home, but was equally clear that he believed that if he stayed in the hospital, he would die and that if he went home, he would begin to swallow again and recover. The doctor sent him home on hospice (a long story for another chapter) and suggested he would be dead in approximately two to three weeks. As I write this chapter, I am happy to report that my dad is still alive and that his body is stronger than it was almost three months ago. He is still struggling with solid foods, but he is getting enough calories in (approximately 1500 per day) to keep him alive. He is interested in watching movies, again and in going for short walks outside. In addition, he is starting to go for rides in the car with one of my sisters and last night went out to dinner with her and her husband. Based on the information from the doctor at the hospital, my father is a walking miracle!! Yet, I am confident in his strength and resilience as he has demonstrated this time and time again to me. Some would argue and say that he "knows he is dying" and that this is his last hurrah. Only our dad and God, or the Spirit, or the Universe, whatever one's belief is, really knows for sure. For now, I choose to put my faith in the idea that our father wants to enjoy life and not be cooped up in his house waiting to die.

It has been a struggle for my sisters and me to get on the same page with what the best care really is for our father. As one can imagine, there are all kinds of family dynamics coming into play. These dynamics go back to childhood. I have become more acutely aware of my role and am choosing to change my behavior. For example, I am choosing to not engage with one of my sisters (with much professional support) who is extremely difficult to deal with, to say the least. Suffice it to say, she believes that she is the only one who knows what is best for our father. Instead of getting into "arguments" with her, I have chosen to not engage at all and to set limits as to how she can engage with me. In addition, I have set limits with my other sister to not share her negative encounters with our difficult sister if she is not willing to do something about it. From a heart-centered approach, all of us want what is best for our dad. However, when one person believes that they are the only one who knows what is best, it never works out well for anyone, especially the patient/family member being cared for.

One coping or navigation tool that I wish to SHOUT out is the importance of putting caregiving desires in writing and having authentic conversations with everyone who will have a role in the process ahead of when they are needed. While our father did designate that we are all to act as his agent as co-medical power of attorney, the language suggests that it is to be unanimous. I am confident, our father did this with the intention that if we had to all agree, it might help us get along better. Unfortunately, it has not had the effect he hoped it would. A better approach would have been for our father to talk about what each of our strengths were and to assign roles accordingly. In my father's case, the big roles are: the hiring and firing of caregivers; medical decisions regarding his medical care; making sure the day-to-day tasks are being handled properly; and financial management. These may, or may not, be similar to the tasks that someone else may need to address, but it is a good bet everyone caring for an aging parent will have to address at least one of these tasks. In addition to encouraging our aging parents to put their wishes in writing, it is important that we put our wishes in writing about what we want should any one of us ever need any kind of caregiving or medical decisions to be made on our behalf. This includes, but is not limited to, making sure a will and trust are in place in addition to putting in place durable medical power of attorney(s) and financial power of attorney(s) and spelling out everything in as much detail as possible. It can be very empowering for everyone. A social worker trained to work with families in these ways can be extremely helpful as can an attorney who specializes in these matters.

In the background of all the "superficial challenges" related to caring for an aging parent, it is important to note that there are losses and grief reactions tied to this role. Throughout our lives, as we are the child, our parents take care of us the best they can with the tools that they have. When the roles reverse and it is our time to care for our aging parent(s), it is a loss for us as the adult children that we are losing our parent in that role. We have to have, or be able to come up with, tools that help us be the best caregivers that we can be. Some of those tools come from what we learned from how our parents cared for us and how we watched them care for their parents and other family members. By the time we find ourselves in the role of caregiver of our aging parent(s), we are most likely part of what has been called the "sandwich generation" caring for our own children, and maybe grandchildren, in addition to caring for our aging parent(s), and ourselves.

In addition, there are a series of losses for us as we learn to navigate our new role as caregiver. There are time issues and constraints that can lead to burnout and our own physical and emotional ailments. The physical demands can be taxing. And, the emotion of watching a parent decline can be horrific if we do not have good coping skills and other adequate resources. We may experience any one, or most likely all of the following emotions throughout the process. All of these "emotional" grief reactions can trigger behavioral pieces as well. We may experience denial/shock/disbelief, anger, bargaining, depression, and acceptance, to name a few. Anger may be at our aging parent, siblings, medical professionals, or even with ourselves. Bargaining is when we say "if only . . . ". The "if only" could be wishing that the aging parent would have had the test they were supposed to have, when they were supposed to have it, as an example. Or it could be, "if only" the parent would have gotten to the hospital sooner or wishing that as the caregiver, a different action was taken. Understandably, we may experience depression. This depression may be sadness or it may rise to the level of a clinical depression based on the circumstances we find ourselves in. Acceptance comes and goes. We do not experience these emotions and the accompanying behavioral reactions in a chronological order but in an order that is logical for who we are, what our life experiences have been, and what coping skills we currently have in our tool box. It is a life-long journey that will continue even after a parent has died. I want to SHOUT out the importance of being in touch with your own grieving capacities. Don't be afraid to reach out for help from a therapist to help process whatever you are experiencing. A therapist or life coach can help guide you through this stage of life's journey.

There are losses for the aging parent, as well! It is a loss for them as they lose their independence and sense of control over their own life. The loss for the aging parent can be physical, financial, intellectual/cognitive functioning, emotional, or all of these as it is for our father. With these losses come a whole series of grief reactions that trigger all the emotions that are previously stated in this chapter. In addition, it can result in our aging parent(s) acting out in a variety of ways: having temper tantrums, increased sleeping to avoid a situation, being careless with finances, and other behaviors that may seem hurtful. Remember, to not take their behaviors personally, though I acknowledge this is not always easy to do. The aging parent is communicating their frustration and sense of loss and grief the only way they know how at the time.

I am choosing to find joy in my life every day and remove myself from a situation that is unhealthy for me and that I know is unhealthy for my father. I may not be able to change the dynamics as it relates directly to my father's care, but I do not have to put myself in the way of harm. That is what I am choosing. All of this is being shared to share with you the importance of self-care and making truly healthy choices for you in difficult situations whether you are the primary caregiver, one of many caregivers, or have the fortune of being able to afford paid caregivers in the home for you or a loved one. So, the next navigation or coping tool I really want to SHOUT out is the importance of self-care.

Caregiving can be a blessing and a curse. It is important that caregivers take care of themselves since caregiving is likely to be a long-term commitment. What that looks like for you, will be different than what it looks like for another family caregiver. Keep in mind, also, what works today, may not work tomorrow. It is important to have a whole tool box, or backpack, full of self-care tools to utilize. For me, what works is walking, gardening, reading, writing, talking it out, meditating (what this looks like for each one of us might be different), and yoga to name a few of my tools. To be fair, some days it feels like nothing is working and then I go through my go-to list and I do feel better. I also schedule therapeutic massages monthly, Reiki sessions with a friend of mine, and time to nap if all else fails. I also have an attorney and a therapist I can talk to. The important point is to create a self-care plan that is reflective of who you are so that burnout and stress does not make it difficult for you to care for your loved one. Reaching out to a social worker or life coach who is trained to support you in your role is very important.

In my role as a social worker, one of my areas of practice is around ethics. I will be sharing some of this information in an effort to provide empowerment on your journey as a family caregiver. The National Association of Social Workers Standards for Social Work Practice with

Family Caregivers of Older Adults, says that a family caregiver can come from within the family of origin, extended family, domestic partners, friends, or other individuals who support an older adult or parent(s). Family caregiving can include a large variety of tasks with the goal of providing supports and services that enhance or maintain an older adult's quality of life. These tasks include:

1. Emotional, social, and spiritual support;
2. Assistance with decision making related to health care, financial matters, and lifespan planning (planning for our life as we age);
3. Assistance with physical tasks, such as bathing, dressing, or walking;
4. Support in navigating and negotiating health and social service systems, such as dealing with health insurance and long-term care insurance;
5. Arranging and overseeing paid helpers in the home, communicating with healthcare professionals, or advocating for quality care and services;
6. Assistance with practical matters, such as housekeeping, processing paperwork, or going to medical appointments and other appointments;
7. Financial support, including direct financial assistance and help with bill-paying;
8. Shared housing.

Caregiving may occur on an intermittent or on-going basis. It may be part or full-time. It may include support from a distance or in the older adult's home or other setting. Family caregiving, here, is primarily referred to as that done on a voluntary basis and not to professional or contractual services that are provided for a fee to the public. (NASW Standards for Social Work Practice with Family Caregivers of Older Adults, National Association of Social Workers, Washington, DC, 2010).

Social work ethics provide some guidelines of things to think about when providing caregiving for an older adult family member. Once such consideration is that of the older adult's right to self-determination. Often, caregivers forget that older adults feel a sense of loss and grief, as previously discussed, as decisions are being made for and about them. The more the older adult can be included in the decision-making process, the better and it helps to decrease episodes of depression and anxiety. Other symptoms of grief that are normal include: increased anger and frustration, a sense of helplessness, a sense of isolation, and difficulty sleeping, to name a few.

Additional resources and support can be found by visiting the National Institute on Aging www.nia.nig.gov/health/caregiving .

You can learn more about Ellen Craine and how she can support you and your family at www.crainecounseling.com or by email at ellen@crainecounseling.com

ELLEN CRAINE

Ellen M. Craine, JD, LMSW -Clinical and Macro, ACSW, is in private practice as a licensed clinical and macro social worker in the State of Michigan. She owns Craine Counseling and Consulting and has over 25 years of experience working with couples, families, groups, and individuals.

Ellen Craine is a relationship and life coach incorporating success principles with her social work experience. She is also a social work business and ethics consultant. Ellen Craine is an effective trainer and educator.

Ellen Craine is a #1 International Bestselling Author of four co-authored books available on Amazon. Signed copies are available through her website.

You can learn more about Ellen Craine and reach out to her to schedule one of her workshops/trainings or individual or group work on her website: www.crainecounseling.com

You can connect with Ellen Craine here:
Facebook group: Living through Loss and Grief
Facebook page: Craine Counseling and Consulting Group.
LinkedIn: Ellen Craine

She can be reached by email at ellen@crainecounseling.com

IT'S OKAY TO SAY "NO"
Getting Used to the Discomfort of Choosing Yourself First

Sarah DeGeorge

Have you said "no" recently? Was it to protect yourself, your energy? How did you feel after?

One word can make all the difference and even though it's just two letters, it has so much power.

The word "no" in its most simple, soft-spoken, one syllable existence doesn't carry much power but when you say it from a place of power within you, the word becomes something different. Even when said in the calmest of tones, a "no" coming from a place within you that requires a need for peace, a desire for change, or simply a place of knowing your "why" and what aligns with that is key to its power.
I have always had a weird relationship with "no" and especially with "yes". You'll learn a lot about how the word "no" can sometimes hurt to receive but also can be powerful and freeing and why "yes" can easily make you feel trapped when you say it too many times.
Whether it's a fear of missing out, a fear of not fulfilling a duty, or

simply a fear of letting someone down, we need to strip away a lot of the emotions around "no" and realize it is a useful tool when it comes to allowing us to ensure our time, space, and self is respected. When we create clear boundaries with "no" then we are able to be presented with more opportunities to say "yes"!

Humble Beginnings of "No"

As a shy and sensitive child, I never wanted to upset anyone or be yelled at, so I tended to avoid the word "no". I can remember times in which "no" was used towards me with such power that it made me immediately cry.

One time, I offered my own thoughts on how to successfully cross a railroad crossing while in preschool and my teacher responded with such an immediate and scathing "no!" that I still can feel my body melting into the floor and tears pooling in my eyes as an adult. Was the answer wrong? Not at all but because it was not what my teacher was looking for, I became embarrassed and afraid to speak up again out of fear of another "no" being hurled towards me.

I vividly remember being a young child in a home video and I am about to knock someone's soda over and the men in the picture collectively yell "no!" at me. Understandably, they were avoiding a mess and potentially soda falling on my tiny head, but I remember being so nervous around that scene in the home video and embarrassed that I would always fast-forward beyond that part.

So, you see, the word "no" has always been a point of contention with me, a word that was used to tell me I was being "bad" or wrong. As an adult, I now know no one can truly hold power over us but "no" can also be a word that can be yielded as power for ourselves as well and I needed to find that clear distinction in life when I was young.

Moving Up in The World of "No's" and "Yeses"
Living life as a teen is already hard enough but when you are carrying a very icky feeling around the word "no," it does make life harder.

For one, I wanted to be seen as cool but also had a very hard time in loud and over-stimulating situations (remember, I've always been super sensitive) so large gatherings were not my favorite place but one I felt I needed to be at to stay "cool" in the eyes of my peers.

I would be so overwhelmed each time I would enter a house with noise, people, and debauchery but felt as though if I said no, I would never be invited again. There were many evenings I wished I could go back and simply state "I'd rather stay in and watch a movie with a friend or two, thanks but NO thanks!"

To be fair, without having experienced what I don't enjoy, I wouldn't have a clear idea of where and what I would rather be doing. In hindsight, I am not mad about not saying no, but I do wish I had said it sooner in social situations.

When I was a teenager, I took a job at a place where I felt very uncomfortable the moment I walked into training. The manager did not realize I was brand new and just assumed I was incompetent when I struggled with their point-of-sales system. Instead of taking time to train me, the manager just talked down to me and told me I was dumb.

The verbal nonsense continued with other snide remarks and to be honest, I had saved up enough from previous jobs that I did not NEED this part-time job. Those first few hours gave me all I needed to know about how misaligned I was from this part-time job and when asked if I would be coming back, I said "no," and made sure to hand in my uniform. Did I feel nervous? Yes, but I also felt weirdly excited for putting myself first and knowing my worth, even at a younger age.

I was able to find another job quickly where I stated a resounding "yes!" to getting hired. I worked there for several years, feeling appreciated and supported by management and making more money.

Were there times in my teen years when I did not have a clear idea of whether something was a resounding no or yes? 100%

I botched soccer tryouts simply because I got in my head and said, "I'm not good enough," so I purposely tripped to make myself look more incompetent in the sport than I was. I couldn't handle not being chosen for my own skill set, so I chose "no," by sabotaging any opportunity for a "yes!"

After soccer tryouts, I tried my hardest to learn my non-negotiables. I learned whether something was or was not for me and I paid more attention to my internal narrative. I asked myself, "Am I afraid of the unknown, or is this truly just not for me?"

No As a Word of Love and Support
Even though I am an adult, hearing or having to say "no" still has that

sting attached to it. Although I have somewhat worked through the ability to discover the meaning behind the "no"- was it from a place of kindness or a place of anger?—I still needed to be taught that distinction through others.

A great example of "no" from a place of kindness was my first opportunity to write for a local paper. My article would have been awesome had it been a press release but as an article, it was missing all the key components. My editor sent back a resounding "no" on this piece I had sent in. Did it hurt? Yes! But, it came from a place of kindness as my editor wanted me to succeed. And so I went back to rewrite it until it sounded less like a media advisory and more like a story. Their "no" became many "yeses" once I got my writing style down.

This is where I learned even saying "no" can be an expression of care and support for someone.

When I say no, I say it because it does not serve me, and it would be unfair to take up the space of someone who would enjoy the position or invitation more than myself.

Diving Into the Power of No
One of the hardest ways I learned to say "no" was during one of the darkest periods of my life.

I was bringing in clients, I was at every networking event, and I was doing all the "right" things I believed I should be doing, but instead of feeling great, I was feeling like a deflated balloon.

I was tired, I was nervous all the time, and while I was moving ahead in life and my career, I almost felt like the world was on fast forward and I was just staring at a screen, sitting stagnant.

Every work email made me nervous; I couldn't focus on the tasks I had for clients AND balance my mental well-being.

I had lost my guiding compass and I was going into deep and choppy waters. The moment I knew I was amid a storm was when I began to lose touch with reality and found myself in a deep psychosis—which is something I will always be very candid and open about. Not because I am ashamed, but because I yes'ed myself into a state of disassociation which was a scary and sad turning point in my fear of no.

With my increasing client list and decreasing free time, I found myself eating more dinners in front of my computer and responding to emails later and later. This did not serve anyone—especially me.

I could have also said no to the endless list of engagements, networking events, and industry get-togethers, but I didn't want to miss out on THAT moment (remember my high school days?), even though I did not enjoy 85% of the places I went and didn't feel a connection to the group or individuals

So then WHY did I do this? Perhaps it was because I thought it was what I should be doing as a professional or a fear of missing out on that next opportunity but I believe it all stemmed from those fears of hearing "no" when I was younger. I did not want to be the person to say "no" and was too exhausted to even begin to remember those moments from my younger years of standing in my growing power as a human!

Now, I was sitting here with my pulse out of control, I could hear my heart in my ears as I began to pull myself back from another panic attack. So much time and anguish could have been saved at this moment had I leaned into the power of "no" because I highly doubt anyone would have missed me at those events.

It took a lot of planning and courage to turn all my "yeses" into healthy, appropriate "nos". I reached out to my network to take on the clients I could no longer handle. Part of healing was realizing that I did not need to stay in the state of pure agony I found myself in- one built on extreme panic, no sleep, and a lot of tears.

"No" was my way out and had I simply remembered those moments from my younger years, I could have used it to develop a stronger work/life balance; even 30 minutes of peace in the morning before work would have allowed space in my life for what mattered most— my family, friends, and a bit of freedom to exist and feel the wind through my air (without my mind wandering to my next work task).

Thankfully, after months of healing, reevaluating, and a lot of help from my family, friends, colleagues, and my therapist (thank you, always!) I was able to slowly rejoin parts of society again. I now have a better understanding of my upper limits and the benefit of saying "no" to events, people, and experiences that don't serve me.

When You Say "No" but WANT To Say "Yes"

So, I've spent so much of this chapter telling you about how to say no but let me throw another angle at you.

You know that feeling you have in your stomach, it can almost be confused for butterflies but it's just your body and your mind telling you that you need to go for it.

Whatever it is, you should go for it if your body is giving you those good feelings toward something.

You might be compelled to say "no" because I have told you in many words prior how it is okay to do so.

But there is a clear difference when no is to hold your power, keep your alignment, and when no is used as the safety net to keep you safe—but not growing. My soccer tryouts are a perfect example of the latter.

Have I said no to things I wanted to say yes to? Absolutely.

I have not taken speaking opportunities, job opportunities, and a plethora of other opportunities, especially in my younger years, out of fear of looking like a failure or because of A LOT of imposter syndrome.

Take a moment to reflect. Think of two moments, one where "no" felt good and one where "no" felt icky and you will see the difference I am trying to convey in this little chapter.

I don't want you to become a "no" person when in reality sometimes it is also okay to say yes (contrary to the title of my chapter).

But remember, you need to tap into yourself, your why, and even your values. You will begin to flex that muscle that will be able to be a great barometer as to whether you are holding true and staying on the path that will lead you to continued growth and greatness by saying no to things that do not serve your purpose or when you are shying away due to fear.

"No" In Your Life, Your Career, and The People Around You

I work in marketing. After my breakdown, I now teach people how to say "no" and also know the difference between when they want to say yes but use no to avoid growth.

My work in marketing is focused on mindfulness and sustainability. You can see from my journey why this is important. I found myself not being mindful and not being sustainable in my own capacity, so I made sure to teach this to small business owners.

We are no longer posting everywhere, only where marketing feels right and where their audience is.

We are no longer working around the clock, we are focusing on times in which we can be present to be a business owner in a marketing capacity (and outsourcing or scheduling out the rest).

I am teaching individuals how to allow marketing to be a part of their business and not let this one piece overtake all other aspects (including off-the-clock time with family or simply eating a meal AT a dinner table).

I have been able to utilize my experience to not only teach others how to do marketing in a sustainable way but to also do it in a way that personal growth and introspection. A side effect of personal evolution is an increasing awareness of when a person needs to say "yes" and when they need to say "no", whether they are working or not.

When we practice "no" when something truly does not serve us, this makes saying no in all aspects of life easier.

"No" can take on many forms, from not taking on new clients to deciding someone is not a good fit to work with. It can mean honoring your unique voice in your industry, despite what your peers are saying or doing.

It makes me smile when a marketing client says, "I actually said no to speaking at an event because the organization did not align with my own values," and really leans into the power of that no. It makes me even happier when that "no" frees up the space for them to get the opportunity they were looking for and follow their guiding light.

When we create that space between what serves us, what will help us grow, and what will keep us stagnant or unhappy, we are able to discern when "no" is appropriate and needs to be said. Once this clarity happens, it becomes so much easier to trust your gut, stand in your power, and say "no, this does not serve me."

Steps To Build Your "No" Muscle
When you really want to dive into your "no" muscle in your life and career, here are some tips to take away:

- Start with small things like saying no to something by yourself. What I found helpful would be to say "no" to a second coffee I want to get while out when I could easily make it at home and save money.

- Move onto a very low-key event or gathering in which no is okay. This could be a larger event for a group you are in or a friend gathering when you just want to stay in (we all have those days).

- Try it out with someone you trust. You can even let them know you are saying no more often so that if an invite comes and you decline, they already know what's coming! This is a good way to showcase how people who care will not be offended and will support a no when you simply cannot get yourself out of the house or it doesn't align with you. For me, this would be a friend inviting me out to a loud bar after 8 pm. None of that sounds enjoyable to me, so a no keeps me safe and aligned.

- No doesn't have to be so outward. If you are overwhelmed at work, instead of a simple "no" you can also showcase this by saying "I do not have the capacity for this right now but can get this to you by tomorrow evening." This can be an easier way to give yourself the time and space to complete tasks.

- Remind yourself that anyone (be it a friend, significant other, or person at work) who is offended by your boundaries or declining an invitation might not be the best person for you to interact with regularly. You ultimately decide this in the end but food for thought!

You know YOU best, don't be afraid to say no!

Also, a quick note to my friends who read my story and edited it! Thank you for saying YES.

SARAH DEGEORGE

S arah is an animal lover, digital marketing specialist, and lover of travel. This is her first published piece in print form, but she has been writing for over a decade in her career as a freelance writer and most of her life as a passion. When she isn't helping her clients with their digital marketing strategy, she is most likely going on a walk, trying out a new restaurant or coffee shop, or trying to put a smile on someone's face somewhere in the world.

You can learn more about Sarah at www.sardegeorge.com
Instagram: www.instagram.com/sardegeorge

IT'S NEVER TOO LATE TO FOLLOW YOUR DREAMS!

My Second Act in Life as a Nurse

Susan DeGeorge

I had always thought about being a nurse when I was 7 or 8 years old. Reading was one of my favorite pastimes and I read about Florence Nightingale and Clara Barton. I read how they made a difference in people's lives by helping them and I wanted to make a difference also.

Math and science were never my favorite subjects in grade school and at Mendham High School. I knew I had to do better in them if I wanted to get into college. I had thought about being a candy striper at the local Morristown Hospital and I knew some HS classmates who volunteered and they enjoyed it a lot. I found that I was really busy with schoolwork, and running cross country in the fall and track in the wintertime. I started to move away from nursing and began to think more about social work. I could still help people, just not in the medical field. I applied to three colleges that had social work courses and got accepted into all three.

My college choice was Juniata College, a small school in Huntingdon, Pennsylvania near Penn State University. A few students from my high school were going there and I had heard good things about Juniata. The good things were all true! I majored in psychology and human interaction and I could design my own major, which attracted me to JC. I went to the May 1980 graduation and got a blank diploma, since I didn't have enough credits to graduate and I had already signed up for summer school. I finished summer school at JC and still needed 6 more credits.

Once the school year was over, I returned home to my parents' home in Brookside and looked for a job so I could make enough money to fund my last semester at Juniata College. I did find a child care position at the Matheny School for Cerebral Palsy Young Adults in nearby Peapack, New Jersey. It was about 25 minutes from my house and I loved driving the wood lined roads. It was on top of a hill and you could see for miles–so pretty! I worked 5 days a week, 7am to 7pm with girls, who were between 10 and 12 years old. I helped them with their daily activities, such as eating, going to the bathroom, and working with them in the classroom. I really enjoyed working with them and I was very sad to leave. I worked there from September 1980 to June 1981 and then I returned to Juniata College for my last semester of college.

My 9 months working at Matheny were very fulfilling and I found that I had made a difference in their lives, which made me very happy. I was thinking that maybe I should have gone into nursing, but Juniata only had a pre- med program for doctors and not nurses. My fear of not doing well in the science courses, such as biology and chemistry kept me from following a nursing career. I needed more confidence in myself. I hoped I would find it soon!

In August 1981 I finally graduated with my BS degree in psychology and I looked around for a job and also for a way to volunteer my time. I got a job at a graphic arts store as a clerk and it was interesting. I had never been exposed to graphic arts or the supplies that were needed. I learned alot and I was able to create a birthday card for my dad and a menu that was used in a play. I saw a newspaper ad that said the local Somerset Hills Hotline was looking for volunteers so I went to their training class. We had about 10 people, of different ages and I enjoyed meeting our fellow volunteers and helping the callers. I let them talk and tried to be non-judgmental. We would give the callers resources to contact and hopefully, they followed up with them. We had callers who were having problems with drugs and depression. Some males only wanted to talk with a female operator, so they could do inappropriate things on the other line and I always felt weird talking with these men. I felt that I was trying to make a difference by helping the callers and I made new friends, while I was living at home with my parents in Brookside NJ.

One of my fellow volunteers, Gene DeGeorge, asked me if we wanted to man the phones together. We did and I enjoyed my time talking to Gene and taking numerous calls. Gene and I became friends, and then we got engaged in May 1985 and married on May 3rd, 1986. Gene helped me discover the field of customer service and I worked at both Atlas Sound in Parsippany, New Jersey and then Thomas & Betts in Bridgewater, New Jersey.

Talking to clients from all over the country was something I enjoyed greatly and in October 1988, Gene and I traveled out to California. We stayed with my middle sister, Gretchen, Steve (her husband), and their infant son, Danny. Disneyland was our destination and we were looking forward to all the rides and attractions. I had talked many times with a buyer from Bisco Industries, Vince, and I let him know about our upcoming trip to Disneyland. He let me know that his office was across the street from Disneyland and we were welcome to use their parking lot. We appreciated Vince's offer and we met him and parked in his lot. We saved $15 dollars and I enjoyed finally meeting him in person. I found I had a good rapport talking with my customers and I had gotten letters of recognition from both my customer service jobs. I felt happy and fulfilled. We had our daughter Sarah on February 28th, 1991 and she was such a cute baby. I enjoyed my 3 months off, taking Sarah for strolls along our country road in Washington, New Jersey and bringing her to meet her relatives.

While on maternity leave from Thomas & Betts, my manager brought up the idea of telecommuting. Gene told me to pursue it and I did, becoming the first telecommuter from Thomas & Betts. Our downstairs office became my work station and they provided the desk and computer and hooked up the phone lines so I could talk to our customers in the Chicago area. I was on 8am to 6pm and I took breaks when Sarah napped or when we went strolling outside. This ideal job lasted until the Spring of 1992, when our company bought another company. I wasn't offered a transfer but we did get a small severance package, which was appreciated. Sarah was 16 months old now and walking everywhere. I was relieved because I knew I couldn't continue the telecommuting job and I wanted to spend more time with Sarah and Gene.

My next job was a part time job at the local Burger King in Washington, New Jersey working 8pm until close, one night a week. I learned to cook, clean the fry stations and the broiler, and take orders . It was fun and I met a lot of older regulars who ate at BK. An elderly man, who delivered medications to local residents from the Washington Pharmacy, was a regular customer and we became friends. He delivered to a woman in Washington who needed help around her home. I contacted the woman and started working with her through United Cerebral Palsy. I worked with her awhile and then took a Certified Home Health Aide Course and passed the written test. I worked with a few different families in the Washington area and I really enjoyed my time with them. One client stood out, she was 91 years old and her husband and sister had passed away. She had no living relatives and I visited her 3 times a week from 8am to 12pm, helping her bathe, eat breakfast and make lunch, and dinner. I worked with her for about a year and then she got really ill and went to the local Warren Hospital in Phillipsburg, New Jersey. She had mentioned once that she wanted to die on her birthday. I visited her on her 92nd Birthday and she was in the intensive care section. Her eyes were closed. I knew that a person's sense of hearing is the last thing that goes so I told her It was her 92nd Birthday!! She had made it!!! I told her that if she was ready to go, she could go. I found out that after I left, another elderly friend came, and then my 92 year old client passed away on her birthday. She had gotten her wish!! I was happy helping the clients and their families. I knew I was in the field that I was meant to be in and it felt right! It might sound funny but I always felt I was born to help people.

In April 1999, Gene was diagnosed with aggressive prostate cancer and he started radiation treatments. I was really frightened that I would lose Gene and Sarah was only 8 years old. Too young to lose her loving dad!

CHHA pay was not enough to survive on and I knew I would need to take an LPN course if I wanted to have a future in the healthcare field. I contacted the Warren County Vo-Tech School and enrolled in the September 2000 LPN course. I was 43 years old at the time and most of my other classmates were between 18 and 30. Our course ran Monday to Friday, 8:30am to 3:30pm. I enjoyed the 11 month course and enjoyed the different subjects that we studied, such as geriatrics, maternity, mental health, and pharmacology. My fear was that being 43 years old, would I retain what I had read?

We did our maternity rotation at Warren Hospital in Phillipsburg, New Jersey and that is where Sarah was born in 1991. I did see the RN who had helped me with Sarah and I was so glad I got to thank her for all her great care that she gave to us!!! I also witnessed a cesarean section and I almost felt like I was going to pass out. I knew maternity nursing was not going to be my specialty!! Our geriatric rotation was at the Warren Haven Nursing Home in Oxford, New Jersey. We interacted with patients who had some dementia and we learned to be patient with them and let them talk. My volunteering on the hotline did pay off!!. We got exposure to different types of nursing when we had a job fair at our Vo-Tech in May 2001. We had representatives from local nursing homes, a home health agency and a developmental disability facility. They explained what jobs we could apply for and I gravitated to the geriatric area. I enjoy hearing the stories that older people tell about their youth and their lives. Graduation came quickly and on August 4th, I graduated with 9 of my fellow nurses. I won an award for having the highest grade point average and for being the most compassionate. My graduation was my 44th Birthday present to myself. I hadn't done as well as I had liked at Juniata College so I was grateful that I did well at my LPN course!!

Credit goes to my family for helping me pass my course. Gene picked Sarah up at her after-school care, since I was still at my course. They gave me time to study when I needed and motivated me when I doubted myself. I applied to a local nursing home, Brakeley Park Care Center in Phillipsburg and I got the job as a Graduate Nurse, since I had not taken my National NCLEX exam yet. My first day on the job was very memorable since it was September 11, 2001 and we were in orientation and also watching the TVs to catch the sad news. Since I couldn't pass medications yet, I worked 7a to 3p and got the residents up, washed, dressed, and ready for their day. I had time to talk with them and get to know them as people. I did enjoy my job and also it gave me more time to study .I took the National LPN test in November 2001 and passed. All of the 10 students in my class passed our National LPN exam and we were the first class to do this. Quite an honor!

My first LPN job was a night 7pm to 7am shift (3rd Floor Long Term Care) at the Brakeley Park Nursing Home in Phillipsburg, about 30 minutes from our home in Washington. I passed meds, did dressing changes, changed colostomy bags, and cleaned up our residents. I had to rearrange my sleep schedule and that was difficult to do. Gene was a trooper and got Sarah off to school and slept by himself most nights. Not being there for my family was really difficult to handle. They would wait for me to get home on holidays, such as Christmas, and we opened our presents at 8am.

The night shift was quiet sometimes but usually it was busy. Someone was always getting out of their bed unaided and that was not a good thing. My supervisor and I had 90 residents and I had 2 aides to help me. My aides were my eyes and ears and I appreciated all their help! I did witness a few deaths and we tried to keep the residents as comfortable as possible. Their family usually was there and we respected their wishes. One resident's passing really stands out in my mind. She was 93 years young, laying in bed, and her relatives and I were there. When the lady passed, her daughter requested for me to open the window and let her mom's spirit out. That request amazed and touched me. I felt honored to help her family feel some relief that their mother's spirit had flown up to Heaven. After two years, I started the 3p to 11p shift and I had 45 residents. I did see a few residents for rehabilitation, after a knee or hip replacement. It was interesting cleaning their surgical areas and keeping them clean. I learned to pace myself and to give each resident my full attention. I enjoyed it for a while but it prevented me from seeing Sarah when she returned from school or having dinner with my family.

After leaving Brakeley Park in February 2008, after six and a half years, I needed a break from my 45 patient workload! I had started a part time second job with a home care agency in 2005 and I had one client at a time. I definitely preferred that one to one ratio.

Matheny School for Cerebral Palsy Young Adults was my much needed relief from my 45 client caseload!! I was so happy to return and see some familiar faces! I remember my first day there and I saw the name of one of the residents who I worked with back in 1980. It was so nice to see this person all grown up and now in his 30's. I really enjoyed my time there and I did switch to another group in 2012. I did recognize another student and the aides I worked with were awesome. We took 2 patients a piece, and we got them ready for bed and then got them up again, dressed, fed them, and ready for their day program.

Pouring and giving medications to 6 patients was a breeze, compared to the nursing home. We took our clients out on trips to restaurants, plays, and proms. We loved the prom and our clients loved getting onto the dance floor in their wheelchairs. Everybody got their picture taken and they felt special!!! I was sad that I had to leave my patients in November 2016 but Gene and I decided to move to our vacation home in Rio Grande, New Jersey. I keep in touch with some of the residents and my staff via Facebook and it feels really good to stay connected!!!

Nursing jobs are easy to find and I signed up with Bayada Nurses a few months before we moved down full time to South Jersey. I had been familiar with Bayada because another client of mine had used them also. Bayada was a well-run agency who treated their nurses well. I worked with a few different cases for 6 years and officially retired in December 2022, after 21 years of nursing. I do fill in occasionally when needed and I enjoy my clients and their families.

Getting into nursing can be done by looking for an LPN Class, usually held at a local community college and it lasts at least a year. An RN degree requires a student to apply to a community college and after 2 years graduate with an Associates' Degree and then take the National RN-NCLEX test. There are so many areas of nursing to look into. Emergency Room Nursing, Oncology, Pediatric, Home Health, Public Health, Geriatric Nursing. If you want to start as a CNA (Certified Nursing Assistant), there are courses given at the local community college night programs or a nursing home might have a course, and then you can work there, after passing your test. I also did work overnight for a few months in correctional nursing, passing out 9pm narcotic meds with a guard escort near Clinton, New Jersey and taking care of the inmates in the infirmary. It was an interesting few months and the prison food we ate was not bad at all!

Nursing has given me a lot of satisfaction and I am so glad I took the chance and started my nursing journey at the ripe old age of 43. I discovered that I was still able to learn and retain the information that I needed for nursing. It was fun to help people and I felt really satisfied!! I am happy to report that most of the nurses in my 2001 nursing class are still LPN's and we have a few RN's too. It's never too late to follow your dreams!

SUSAN DEGEORGE

S usan Hoadley DeGeorge is a 66 year old woman who enjoys reading, gardening, traveling to new places, and finding interesting recipes to try. She is the proud mom of Sarah and the proud wife of Gene DeGeorge for the past 37 years. Susan began her LPN nursing career at 44 years old in 2001 and just retired in December 2022. She enjoys living near the South New Jersey shore and loves walking along the bay, looking for sea glass. She has 2 full jars and is working on her 3rd.

If you have any questions about Nursing or anything else, please contact Susan at degeorgesusan@yahoo.com

EMBRACING GROWTH AND FREEDOM
Letting Go of the Past

Adrianne Fekete

As human beings, we are constantly evolving intellectually and spiritually. The journey of personal growth is marked by the ability to embrace change and not let our past define us. In a recent summit, I spoke about the importance of letting go of the past and forging ahead towards a better future. It really stopped me in my tracks and I decided to take a peek into my past. It was not to dwell on anger, sadness, or regret… it was to see how far I have come in my journey.

At 10, I got my first taste of being an entrepreneur & I kid you not I truly knew this was my journey.

At 14, I was told I couldn't do things because of my gender.

At 17, My guidance counselor told me, "You are not smart. You will never amount to anything. You don't have the marks or the money to go to college or university. Go and marry rich, have a few kids, and you'll be fine."

Those words fuel me to this day because for me: REJECTION TRULY IS REDIRECTION.

At 19, I opened my first business and sold it 5 years later for a profit.

At 24, I started a PR agency & served clients such as the Rolling Stones, U2, Colin Farrell & the WWE. This required a certain amount of executive protection so…

At 30 something, I became the first woman in Canada to own a fully licensed, private investigations & security business.

I firmly believe looking back at our achievements and how far we have come can be a powerful tool in defining our identity. Instead of limiting ourselves based on past experiences, we should use them as stepping stones towards growth and self-discovery. Our past does not have to hold us back; it can serve as a foundation on which we build our present and future.

Drawing from my own life experiences, overcoming rejection and adversity, proving that I was capable of achieving success despite being told otherwise: these experiences fueled my determination to persevere and led to several milestones in my journey.

Forgiveness is another key aspect that I place a lot of on. In my opinion, we all make mistakes and experience failures along the way. However, dwelling on these past mistakes does not serve any purpose.

Rather than defining our present or future, we should learn to forgive ourselves and consciously make the decision to change our experiences. I believe that we have the power to shape our own destiny, no matter how many times we might fall.

For example, let's say you set a goal for yourself. If it is an achievement, deadline, whatever it is, you set the goal. Right? Move the date forward, revise your achievements and most importantly, please don't be so hard on yourself. Speak kindly to yourself. Love yourself enough to forgive yourself for not making it and look at what you can do to still hit that goal. The power of forgiveness and the ability to change our goals and timelines has been so incredibly empowering for me. By taking ownership of our own stories and refusing to let negative experiences define us, we can embrace personal growth and change more effectively.

For me, living in the present moment and acknowledging personal growth is essential. By being mindful of our progress and counting our blessings, we can develop a more positive outlook on life. Viewing past mistakes as lessons and opportunities for growth rather than tragedies allows us to embrace the present and look forward to the future with renewed enthusiasm. Through mindfulness I have learned to appreciate the challenges I have faced because through them I have developed resilience and gratitude which has led to a more fulfilling life.

For those of you who are struggling, or wanting to change something in your life, my message here is very simple: Your mindset ultimately revolves around the importance of staying true to yourself as well as leading with kindness and forgiveness. I cannot emphasize enough external influences and negative experiences should not define who we are today or tomorrow, and it is definitely not how our story ends. Every struggle we face is merely a chapter in our larger narrative, and it is up to us to determine its significance. My mantra, "yes you can," encapsulates my belief in the power of determination and the ability to overcome any obstacle.

You are one decision away. Embrace your journey of personal growth and freedom, with curiosity and confidence in the knowledge that we have the power to shape our own destinies.

"You have always had the power my dear. You just have to learn it yourself." ~ The Wizard Of Oz

ADRIANNE FEKETE

A drianne Fekete is a storyteller, podcaster, publisher, and private investigator on a mission to break the bias, one rockstar at a time. As a thought leader and a pioneer in a male-dominated industry, she knows firsthand what women can face. Adrianne believes in the power of the pack, so she built a group of rockstar women who are here to mentor, inspire, and teach. She is developing a platform dedicated to globally elevating feminine values, reaching multiple women and leaders within all industries, as well as leaving the world a kinder place. The struggle is part of the story.

Follow Adrianne Fekete:
YouTube: youtube.com/@iamunbreakable

Apple Podcast: podcasts.apple.com/us/podcast/i-am-unbreakable/id1669941557

Instagram: www.instagram.com/i.amunbreakable

LinkedIn: www.linkedin.com/in/adrianne-f-a6800114

TikTok: www.tiktok.com/@i.am.unbreakable

Facebook: www.facebook.com/adriannefekete?mibextid=LQQJ4d

Twitter: twitter.com/AdrianneFekete

IT'S OKAY TO ASK FOR HELP
Why You Should Hire a Pro and Get Out of Your Way

Amy Garelick

Dearest colleagues of the great Generation X. Please allow me to (ahem) step up on my soapbox for a second. **It's Okay to Ask for Help.**

In the heart of every Gen X woman lies a spirit of resilience, a drive that says, "I've got this." We've witnessed the dawn of the digital age, the evolution of pop culture, we've raised families, climbed the corporate ladder, and started businesses. We've been conditioned to believe in the power of self-reliance, often diving headfirst into challenges with an eagerness to prove our worth.

It's fine. Let's flashback to that time you decided to cut your own bangs, only to be met with results that were far from the desired. Or that time when you decided that you could be your own bookkeeper, or social media maven, or a million other DIY moments. How'd that go? Seriously, how did that really go?

Often, the allure of the DIY approach is the desire to save time and money. It's tempting: why seek external help when the internet is free & AI exists? Achieving results without incurring additional costs can be enticing. However, there's an underlying question we often overlook: **What is the true value of our time?** While we might save dollars in the short run, time spent, coupled with potential missteps, and the stress of navigating the unfamiliar, outweighs any savings.

Timing is Everything. When things don't go as planned, the immediate reaction might be to call in the experts to salvage the situation. However, that is like treating a symptom without understanding the disease. Professionals offer more than just solutions to problems; they provide foresight, strategy, and a holistic view of challenges. Their value isn't in merely patching up issues but in crafting a well-thought-out strategy from the onset. It's the difference between reactive and proactive. One offers a temporary fix, the other ensures long-term success.

But What About the Robots? In today's rapidly advancing technological landscape, AI (Artificial Intelligence) stands out as a beacon of potential. But without human optimization, its capabilities are guaranteed to be underutilized. For AI to provide impact, it requires the expertise of those who understand its nuances and how to mold it effectively to serve our real-world needs.

In Conclusion, when life throws you a curveball, and trust me, it will, I challenge you, my fellow Gen X'er, to tap into your superpowers. Strength, adaptability, evolution, and the ability to truly realize the value of your time and energy. Call upon your tribe of experts and let them lead the way.

Where trust meets expertise, success will follow.

AMY GARELICK

Masterful storyteller & dynamic founder/CEO of POWER UP, Amy has channeled her diverse career experience into fostering creative content creation with effective strategies. With 15+ years at Disney Media & Special Events, today, she effectively uses that expertise to infuse marketing pixie dust into her client experiences.

Amy has further evolved her portfolio by incorporating a Certified Content Coaching program, a framework shaping the future of marketing & sales content.

Amy is a disrupter, cementing her reputation as a forward-thinking leader in her field.

When she isn't working with clients, she cherishes every moment spent with her husband Kenny, two sons, Colin & Ryan, & rescue Chihuahua, Princess Leia.

Links:
LinkedIn: www.linkedin.com/in/amygarelick
LinkedIn: www.linkedin.com/company/powerupvideo
YouTube:
www.youtube.com/channel/UCIsEZaLPEwDcYMnbFc8YWvQ

YOUR EXTRAORDINARY LIFE IS WAITING FOR YOU!
You Have the Power to Transform Your Life Into Something Extraordinary

Kelly Geisler

Deep within every person lies the potential to live an extraordinary life. If you find yourself reading this chapter, know this message is meant for you. Your life is ready for transformation, and stumbling upon this chapter is no coincidence.

To receive the most from this chapter, I invite you to read it slowly, participate, reflect, and explore. Allow the transformation to occur by acknowledging what cracks open and accepting what wants to shift. Your soul led you to this moment, so lean back, be curious, and explore all the possibilities before you.

YOU ARE THE CREATOR OF YOUR LIFE
Let's begin by embracing a transformative core belief that can reshape your life into something extraordinary. Everyone can consciously reshape their circumstances and create a life according to their desires.

Yes, you have the power and control to change and create the life you desire. You are the architect of your life. Does this resonate with you?

I understand if you're uncertain about embracing this perspective. You may have felt more like a passenger in your life's journey than the driver. There may have been instances when you've coasted on autopilot, letting the winds steer your course. There might have been times when you inadvertently let others steer, only to find yourself frustrated by the destination.

Today presents an invitation to you to change that narrative. I encourage you to hop back into the driver's seat, grab hold of the steering wheel, and start your extraordinary journey. It's always possible to make the shift and create the life you deeply desire.

MAKING THE SHIFT

The shift toward living an extraordinary life begins with recognizing your life's journey is not a fixed path, but an ever-evolving process that you can design. You have the power to shape your own life, make choices, and have experiences that align with your deepest desires, what feels like the most authentic expression of who you are and what you desire to experience.

Embracing the truth that you are powerful and can change your life will allow you to break free from the stagnation of routine and conformity: which opens a world of soul-aligned possibilities. You are not confined to the box your family or society put you in. You have the power to create and design your box; you've just forgotten how powerful you are.

You see, living an ordinary life is a draining experience. When you find yourself doing things you don't enjoy, being in relationships that don't fulfill you, and going through the motions without genuine excitement, it can feel like the joy is being sucked out of your existence; you're merely living like a robot on autopilot. Over time, living in such a robotic manner can lead to a loss of motivation, a lack of enthusiasm, and even feelings of hopelessness. I have seen too many people live a life that is draining their well-being, which is my inspiration for writing this chapter.

It's essential to recognize the signs of this discontent and take steps to reclaim your life's direction. Remember, you have the power within you to create an extraordinary life. Are you ready to start now?

STEP 1: CLARIFY
I continue to refer to the life you desire as an extraordinary life. Still, I'm curious, what does an extraordinary life mean to you? I invite you to pause and reflect. Be bold and brave and explore what an extraordinary life could look, feel, or sound like for you.

Remember, this is your first opportunity to reclaim your power and the driver's seat. Step beyond the limitations others have placed on you, limitations of what is and isn't possible and explore your definition of an extraordinary life!

The definition is different for everyone; there is no one-size-fits-all. However, for a spark of inspiration, I will share what an extraordinary life means to me. An extraordinary life is deeply rooted in authenticity, connection, heart, purpose, and passion.

AUTHENTICITY

At the core of an extraordinary life is being true to yourself – that's authenticity. It's not about pretending; it's about sticking to your beliefs and values, even when things get tough—being authentic means knowing yourself so well that you're comfortable with your uniqueness. It's about embracing yourself instead of avoiding what makes you special.

When you've formed this strong and honest connection with yourself, your interaction with life and the world reflects who you truly are. You feel vibrant, acknowledged, and respected just for being you. And the best part? You realize that deep down, you're more than enough. You can create an extraordinary life and you deserve it.

CONNECTION

An extraordinary life is not one lived in isolation. To live an extraordinary life, one must cultivate these three most important connections: the connection to yourself, your higher power, and those around you.

Living an extraordinary life is not about shying away from solitude; it's about spending time with yourself as you genuinely enjoy your own company. Recognize that solitude is like soul food, nurturing introspection, and self-compassion. You can genuinely engage with life's richness when your cup is full!

Additionally, forging a meaningful connection with your Higher Power adds support and cultivates resilience in your life. This connection builds a deeper sense of trust and faith, a supportive foundation when facing fear or uncertainty.

Lastly, nurturing meaningful relationships and being part of a community adds depth and richness to your life. The people who share your journey infuse it with diverse experiences that make each day more meaningful!

HEART
Choosing to live from the heart creates profound meaning in every moment. Living from the heart is about approaching life with compassion, empathy, and kindness for others and yourself. Embracing a heart-centered approach means being genuine in all interactions.

This authenticity and heart-centeredness attracts real connections and experiences that create ripples of positive impact, turning ordinary interactions into extraordinary relationships.

PURPOSE
You are an absolute original! There's only one version of you in this world, and that's no accident. You've been gifted with unique talents and abilities that hold tremendous value. Your life's purpose is to embrace and utilize these unique qualities to make a positive impact and contribute to humanity.

When you have a clear purpose, every step you take becomes more meaningful, leading you toward a greater sense of fulfillment and satisfaction. So, go ahead and wholeheartedly embrace what sets you apart. Let this be your guiding star, and you'll witness life unfolding in ways you never imagined – vibrant, dynamic, and rich with meaning.

PASSION

Passion is the last ingredient to creating an extraordinary life. Passion is about understanding what you genuinely resonate with. Seek out the things that ignite such a fire within you that you jump out of bed each morning, propelled by a surge of energy bursting at the seams.

Your passions are little hints from the Universe, leading you toward what truly matters. So, go on, lean into what sets your soul on fire! Here's the secret sauce… when your purpose and passion collide, the magic truly unfolds in life.

STEP 2: RECLAIM YOUR POWER

Doing the inner work isn't always easy, but it is always rewarding. Grab a pen and paper, take a moment to reflect, and identify a situation in your life you wish to change. Bravely confront what is causing unhappiness and dissatisfaction in your life. What desperately needs to be disrupted because you are no longer willing to live with it? I invite you to be bold and vulnerable; keep this situation in mind as you explore the remainder of this chapter.

As you begin this next section, note that you are about to plant the seeds of change that will shift you away from unhappiness and dissatisfaction; leading you toward a life filled with excitement, possibility, and happiness. So, now let's begin this empowering process together!

RECLAIM YOUR RELATIONSHIP WITH LIFE ITSELF

Have you ever heard the saying, "Life isn't happening to you, it's happening FOR you"? This powerful notion suggests you are not a mere victim of circumstance. But somehow, life is supporting you. Although it may seem like you lack control over your life and that adverse events keep piling up, the truth is that life is unfolding in a way that presents you with soul lessons for your growth and evolution, ultimately enriching your human experience—if you allow it.

Life is genuinely working in your favor. The question is, do you agree?

This belief serves as the initial invitation to shift your perspective and relationship with life. You can decide what you believe: Is life unfolding for your benefit or merely happening to you, and you have no control over the experience?

Now let's continue to grow this concept. I want to add another phrase to this statement: "Life isn't happening to you, it's happening for you, WITH you." Even if your experiences feel like life is happening to you and you keep getting knocked down when you try to rise, remember you possess the ultimate power of choice. You can perceive life as a positive, soul-supporting, growth-oriented experience or as a negative, limiting experience. Despite all its challenges, the way you relate to life remains always within your control.

In other words, you have the power to decide whether life is happening for you—offering opportunities for growth and fulfillment—or whether it is happening to you—leaving you feeling powerless and defeated. What belief do you hold? Is there an opportunity to shift your belief? Could you be curious enough to continue to explore this concept with me?

Even during difficult times, remember that you can shape your perspective. You can consistently subscribe to life-affirming beliefs and choose to walk a path with a sense of empowerment, resilience, and openness to life's lessons. Making these choices is how life happens WITH you. By embracing the truth that you are a creator of your reality through the perspectives you hold, beliefs you subscribe to, and aligned actions you take, you can unlock a transformative mindset that will guide you toward a more enriched and purposeful existence.

A PERSONAL STORY

Allow me to share an example from my life that illustrates the transformative power of our choices. Several months ago, I found myself in a traumatic car accident coinciding with a time when everything in my life seemed to fall joyfully into place. In the aftermath of the trauma, I faced a critical decision; how do I approach this experience? It was within my power and control to perceive this experience as life-affirming or life-negating; this typically happens subconsciously. However, I have done enough work coaching myself and others to know it was my responsibility to decide how I would orientate to this new experience. Reaffirming my choice to view this as a growth opportunity would serve me well.

I could have chosen to see myself as a victim, feeling defeated and victimized by the Universe. I could have succumbed to the belief that just when things were finally going well, the Universe knocked me down (again) as if I didn't deserve all the good things happening in my life. This choice may have led me to believe that pain, struggle, and exhaustion were my destiny merely because I've experienced much evidence to support this belief structure. However, I knew I could still choose a different way of relating to this experience.

Amidst the pain and trauma, I made a different choice to believe this experience happened to guide and fuel my soul's evolution, personal growth, and overall betterment. I held to my core belief that life continuously unfolds for my benefit, even in challenging times. Life or the Universe (I use both interchangeably) supports me and is rigged in my favor. I have faith and trust in the Universe without knowing how or why because I believe it is inherently good.

This accident became an invitation—the trauma, an undeniable force—to slow down and take stock of my life; it provided a moment of recalibration, prompting me to reevaluate my priorities and the direction of my life. Was I in alignment with what I truly desired for my life, or was I out of alignment? During this period of reflection, I had an epiphany. I had been missing out on the simple joys and the sweetness of life because I was relentlessly focused on reaching the next goal, driven by a feeling of not having enough. I hadn't realized that I was already living the life I truly desired, my extraordinary life, because I was constantly focused on more money, more freedom, and more joy (this is lack consciousness).

This wake-up call (recalibration) made me fully understand and appreciate that many of my dreams, intentions, and desires had already come true, yet, I hadn't even noticed or enjoyed these manifestations.

Only when I slowed down and took the time to embrace the present moment did I truly recognize the magnitude of what I had created. Through this new lens, I could share deep, heart-felt gratitude with the Universe for showing me what I hadn't been able to see for myself.

From that point forward, this profound perspective shift transformed how I approached my life. I began to live more mindfully while cherishing each moment and savoring the journey rather than racing towards an elusive destination. I began letting go of experiences I wasn't passionate about. The accident, which initially seemed like a setback, became an invaluable catalyst for my personal growth, reminding me to live in harmony with the flow of life. Creating evidence once again that life is supporting me; it is happening FOR me and WITH me. I am the creator of my extraordinary life, just as you are the creator of yours.

STEP 2: RECALIBRATE YOUR BELIEFS

Now, let me share with you another golden nugget. This potent insight will empower you to create your reality, to be the driver of your extraordinary life. As I mentioned earlier, life is not only happening for you but also happening with you; it all begins with your beliefs.

You possess the incredible power to choose your beliefs. I want to shout this concept from the rooftops - you can subscribe to whatever belief you desire. Growing up, you were exposed to your familial, societal, and cultural beliefs that you subconsciously agreed with. Often these beliefs kept you small, helped you believe you weren't good enough, your needs didn't matter, or that you were a burden to others. I want to remind you, as an adult, you don't have to believe something someone else told you to believe or was role-modeled for you to believe. The choice is yours!

In any given moment or situation, pause to identify what beliefs you are currently holding. Remember when I asked you about a situation you wanted to change? Now is the time to work with that situation. What beliefs are you subscribing to as it relates to this situation?

Next, consider what new beliefs you wish to adopt. This is the moment of empowerment; you can actively choose the beliefs that serve your growth and well-being. Ask yourself, in this situation, what belief will empower me? Do I want to believe that life is supporting me? Do I want to believe this experience is happening for my personal growth?

Again, reflect on the situation you wish to change. What beliefs are you currently subscribing to? Be honest with yourself, acknowledge whether your beliefs are empowering or limiting, and then decide what you want to believe instead. This is a transformative moment where you hold the key to changing your life and circumstances.

By deliberately choosing empowering beliefs, you can shape your reality. This might not happen overnight, but with persistence and belief in your ability to create your reality, you'll start to notice positive shifts and new opportunities unfolding before you; this is when your life recalibrates. Your beliefs are the foundation upon which your reality is built, so seize this moment to empower yourself and embrace the change you desire by subscribing to new, life-affirming beliefs.

STEP 3: REALIGN YOUR THOUGHTS, EMOTIONS, AND ACTIONS

Once you have recalibrated your beliefs, it's time to observe your thoughts, emotions, and actions, for they are the other critical components to living your extraordinary life.

Take a moment to notice whether your thoughts align with your beliefs about the situation you want to change. What, specifically, are your current thoughts? Do your thoughts align with your beliefs? By recognizing misalignments, you can consciously shift your thought patterns to be more in line with your beliefs. What new thoughts can you adopt to better align with your beliefs?

Next, shift your attention to your emotions—do your emotions align with your thoughts and beliefs? Do you feel it is possible or impossible for your beliefs to be true?

Quantum Physics and the Law of Vibration state that every thought, action, and belief carry a unique vibrational frequency. The Law of Attraction states like frequencies attract like frequencies. Vibrational alignment is essential to create your extraordinary life.

If you find yourself out of alignment, this is your opportunity to do the inner work. Techniques like Emotional Freedom Technique (EFT), Transformational Life Coaching, and Somatic Therapies can be powerful tools to recalibrate your thoughts and emotions.
Lastly, reflect on your actions. Are your actions in alignment with your beliefs, thoughts, and emotions? Do your actions support your beliefs, thoughts, and emotions, or are they the opposite of what you desire? If your actions are not in alignment, be willing to hold yourself accountable and make the necessary changes. This alignment of beliefs,

thoughts, emotions, and actions is a powerful step toward manifesting the changes you desire in your life.

CONCLUSION

In this chapter, we've explored three game-changing concepts. Firstly, always remember that you have the power to shape your reality, so make it extraordinary. Secondly, foster a relationship with life itself; ask yourself, does life support or oppose you? The power to choose, lies within you. Lastly, work with your beliefs, thoughts, emotions, and actions – these are the key components that shape your reality. Are they aligned with your desired life? If not, let this misalignment spark change, inviting you to start doing the inner work, for your extraordinary life eagerly awaits.

KELLY GEISLER

Kelly Geisler, also known as the Butterfly Guide, is a Certified Transformational Life Coach and Spiritual Mentor, who facilitates profound life changes for her clients. She empowers clients to realize their potential and make bold shifts to align with their authentic desires. By integrating mindset techniques such as Emotional Freedom Technique with spiritual mentorship, Kelly's compassionate approach ensures lasting transformation. With years of experience, Kelly empowers her client's to navigate life's challenges in alignment with their core beliefs and values, make bold changes, and embrace their individuality so they can live a life they truly desire.

Contact Kelly:
Website: www.TheButterflyGuide.com

TikTok: @TheButterflyGuide

YOU ARE HERE TO LIVE BY YOUR OWN LIGHTS
Trust Yourself

Daneika Glenn

"I didn't feel safe."

Those were the words I had spoken out loud for the first time at age 38.

I was standing in my dining room, clutching a copy of The Artist's Way in my hands, and lost in my thoughts over an exercise I had completed from the book.

Suddenly, a jolt of electricity sprinted through my body like the unexpected sound of thunderclaps interrupting a calm, sunny day.

I finally had the clarity and awareness that had been missing all of these years.

All of the doubts and the reasons why began to click and connect in my mind.

All of the pain I felt from not belonging, especially in my family of origin, and the feeling of unfulfillment and meaninglessness made sense.

I had been taught it wasn't safe to be myself.

What I truly wanted and desired to create was outside of the scope of possibility for some members of my family of origin, and they made sure to let me know whenever my dreams were too big for them to hold.

And because of that constant pushback, I chose self-betrayal as a way to belong.

Instead of trusting my perceptions and intuitions, I decided to get involved in the business of "being good" to belong.

Being good meant:

Being good to others at my own expense, minding other people's business instead of my own, and believing other people's stories about who I was and who I wasn't.

What I like to call people-pleasing, self-sabotage, and internalized negative self-talk.

I had been giving away my power, and I wasn't even aware of it until that flash of insight in my dining room that day.

I had been awakened from my dream state that had caused me so much pain in the past.

And now there was no turning back.

I knew what I had to do, and why I had to do it.

I could no longer disregard my own inner wisdom as a way to feel safe or downplay my ambitions to make others feel less threatened.

It was no longer about them, what they thought, or their version of reality.

It was about me healing my relationship with myself by letting go of who I thought I had to be, and trusting myself enough to express all of the truths inside of me, unapologetically.

Learning how to stand in the truth of all that I am and aspire to be is how I found the safety, clarity, and confidence to show up and engage and express all of myself in this adventure known as my life.

And this is what I want for you.

To help you find your way, your truth, and your power to create and become all that you are meant to be.

So, I want to offer you six personal stories to help you do just that.

1. Notice what drains your energy and steer clear of it
When I started my career as a flight attendant, it was very aligned with

several of my core values, including: independence, connecting with new people, having a flexible schedule, and the ability to travel the world.

But the time came when it no longer aligned with who I was becoming, and this misalignment started to show up in a few, noticeable ways.

The first sign was in my attitude.

I started to notice a pattern of feeling resentful, annoyed, and drained just by the thought of returning to work after having time off.

The joy was gone and boredom had set in.

I had outgrown the job, but I wasn't ready to admit it to myself, so the universe started sending me stronger signals in the form of feeling drained physically.

I can remember working twelve-hour days and feeling physically exhausted, unless I was on my last leg of a flight heading home. I would go from yawning, heavy-eyed, and struggling to maintain my energy levels to get through a beverage service, to suddenly catching a second wind the closer the plane got to landing in Minneapolis.

I would miraculously turn into the energizer bunny who breezed through the last beverage service before landing with humor, grace, and enthusiasm.

There were stronger nudges from the universe that eventually turned into pushes before I got the message and courage to leave.

But the day came when I faced my fears and let go of who I was.

My energy levels and attitude improved drastically.

The consistent feeling of your energy being depleted and having a bad attitude is always a sign it's time to move on.

You don't have to do something about it right away. Start by noticing how you feel energetically in different situations and with different people.

And ask yourself:
- Who drains my energy?
- What types of environments drain my energy?

2. Have the courage to follow your intuitive hunches
Back in 2009 I had a strong desire to move to Seattle.

I have always been drawn to the west coast because of its natural beauty, and I was looking for a new career opportunity.

I conducted some preliminary research on housing costs, climate, and income potential and was even more excited by the idea of living in Seattle.

I booked a weeklong trip to get a feel for the city.
Shortly before departing for my trip, I had an intuitive hunch I would meet someone in Seattle who would connect me to a new career

opportunity.

I had no idea how I would meet this person or what they would look like, but I trusted we would cross paths, headed to Seattle, and did meet the person I had a hunch about.

One morning I was on a boat tour of the Puget Sound and Lake Washington with several people.

As we were departing from downtown Seattle, I was struck by the beauty of the view.

An endless expanse of water as far as I could see, and the sun beaming brightly on the downtown skyline.

I wanted to capture the moment, so I asked a woman nearby if she would take a photo of me and the person I was with.

She said yes.

After taking a few photos of us, I thanked her and we started talking.

I told her about my desire to move to Seattle and start a new career, and she said she could offer me a job once I moved to Seattle.

She gave me her card and we said our goodbyes and went back to enjoying the sights of the tour.
I didn't end up moving to Seattle, but my intuition was correct.

You don't have to know how help will arrive, but if you get the intuitive message that it will, have the courage to follow it.

3. Use travel as a way to deepen self-knowledge and spark change

I remember the first time I went to Rome, Italy.

I assumed the Romans would have the same beliefs, perceptions, standards and ideas of what it meant to live the good life as me.

They would value things like working hard to be successful and independence.

Yes, I was that naïve and completely unaware of my cultural conditioning as an American, and I was in for a very pleasant surprise.

Here is what I discovered.

Romans love to luxuriate.

I observed them doing things like taking leisurely strolls with friends during "business" hours and casually conversing and laughing with friends over lunch dates that lasted a few hours.

I also discovered three-hour lunch siestas was the norm for Romans, as well as eight-week paid summer vacations.

Romans take great pride in indulging in pleasure and enjoying their lives now and there were bold displays of this everywhere I went.

They didn't seem to worry or feel guilty about slowing down and delighting in the pleasures of everyday life.

Did I mention they did this while dressed-to-the-nines?

This way of being in the world did not register as a possibility for me prior to visiting Rome.

I was raised with true Midwestern values, believing working hard was a top priority and the early bird catches the worm.

The idea of prioritizing my own pleasure and enjoyment of life first seemed irresponsible.

I had never seen a business owner close their shop for a three-hour lunch break, let alone take eight weeks of vacation every year.

It was inspiring and mind-expanding.

I wanted their lifestyle.

I wanted to relax, experience more pleasure and enjoyment in my everyday life, have time to really connect with the people who matter to me, and look good while doing it.

Traveling to new lands and experiencing new cultures creates contrast and a deeper understanding of who you are and how your experiences and cultural conditioning have shaped your view of the world, for better or worse.

It also gave me the possibility to choose a new way of being in the world based on my desires, not what I had been conditioned to believe was desirable.

Traveling to Rome allowed me to start saying yes to new adventures without the guilt and worry I had been conditioned to feel for wanting to have fun and enjoy my life.
- What do you desire?
- Who do you want to be?

Explore as many new places as possible because it will help let go of who you think you have to be and open you up to who you would truly love to be.

4. Pay attention to your daydreams
I can remember talking with a friend in a restaurant on a brisk New Year's Eve in Minnesota.

I was describing one of my daydreams of being on the beach in Nice, France.
I was captivated by the images in my mind of swimming at this beach with the white-washed rocky coastline protruding from a cobalt sea.

I described what I was wearing and how I felt.

I became so obsessed with this beach that I saved an image of it (the Cote d'Azur) on my laptop.

I didn't make a plan to get there, but on some level, I knew I would get there.

The images were too vivid and real in my mind.

About 18-months later it became a reality when I became a flight attendant.

I ended up spending the day swimming in the cobalt sea with the white-washed rocky coastline just like I had envisioned.

Your daydreams are there to offer guidance and clarity around what you are here to do or experience.

Take them seriously.

5. You are what you see. Make sure you like your reflection
I remember glancing at a piece of artwork I had hanging in my dining room back in 2015.

It had been there a couple of years.
It was a painting that showed a few couples walking down a street on a rainy, overcast day, and there was one woman walking alone behind everyone else.

I was strongly attracted to the painting when I purchased it.
But standing in my dining room that day, it didn't seem to belong any longer.

I wanted to take it down, and I did, but I didn't understand why until I came across a book from Thomas Moore called Care Of The Soul.

According to Moore, our homes are a reflection of our inner-worlds, our subconscious minds.

The story we tell ourselves about ourselves, who we are, who we are not, what we are allowed to have or experience, what we are worthy of, or not worthy of are often unconscious and hiding in plain sight throughout our homes as the objects we fill them up with.

This made perfect sense to me.

I was attracted to the painting because I had been that woman walking alone a few years prior.

I had felt like I was following behind everyone else and I wasn't happy about it.

At that time in my life, I had felt sad, heavy and a sense of drudgery about my everyday life, and those emotions were expressed in the painting through the rainy and overcast day.

That insight from Moore also caused me to take a closer look at the items I had in my house and ask questions.

Questions like, did the items I had in my home reflect my dreams, desires, and aspirations or did they hold me to a past that made me feel sad, disempowered, or trapped?

This questioning led to the removal of other items like clothes, pictures, books, dishes, and shoes.

I started selecting new items for my home with more care and attention to detail.

Going through this process helped me consciously realize how I saw myself, and empowered me to make new choices based on who I wanted to be.

If you are struggling to define what you want or feel stuck in your own life and aren't sure why, spend some time playing detective around your own home. Here are a few questions you can ask yourself.

- What does the artwork and/or photos hanging on your walls tell you about yourself? About your relationships with others? Do you like what you see? Why or why not?
- Are there old, broken, and outdated objects in your home? If so, in what ways is your behavior and thinking old, broken, and outdated?

Making your unconscious beliefs about yourself conscious allows you to remove the items that keep you anchored to a past you no longer want to live in.

6. *Close the door on "what was" to invite in "what could be"*

In 2011, I received an invitation to become a more expanded version of myself via a career change.

I was offered a job at a major airline and I was very excited and afraid.

Afraid, because it meant I would have to leave behind everything I'd ever known and loved up to that point in my life.

I had to find a new home for my cats, sell my car, sell my furniture, move to a new state where I didn't know a soul. On top of that, I had to complete six weeks of a college course work ahead of schedule in order to focus and pass the intense, fourteen hour day training, that would take two months to complete.

And I had about six weeks to complete this entire process and move to Atlanta for two months.

Did I mention I was a full-time college student, I needed to repaint the entire master bedroom and bathroom, go shopping for specific wardrobe specifications, and I didn't have the money to do it?

I was so afraid I wouldn't be able to do it, but the desire for a new life pulled me along, so I started closing the door on what my life had been prior to this new invitation.
I posted my car for sale on Craigslist, and had several interested buyers within hours of the post, and the same thing happened with my furniture.

My aunt agreed to take two of my cats, and miraculously, my mom just happened to be heading out of state to her house at that time and agreed to drop them off.

It all seemed to be magically coming together to push me into this new life.

I was able to complete all of the tasks and move to Atlanta as scheduled, but I had to close the door on my life as it was in order to walk through a new door, an unknown world of new opportunity.

I ended up working in the airline industry for about ten years.

I had the opportunity to make so many of my dreams come true, like vacationing in Australia for a few weeks, snorkeling for the first time in Costa Rica, living in New York City, attending my first Broadway Play, visiting India, bike riding through Barcelona, take my first cruise to the Caribbean, and still have enough time off to create a loving, adventurous-filled relationship with another human being.

Looking back now, it was one of the best decisions I've ever made, but make no mistake about it, it was one of the hardest, too.

I was so sad at the time about what I had to leave behind and close the door on.
What door would you be willing to close if you dared to believe everything you wanted was on the other side of your fear?

Summary
You are here to live by your own light by expressing the truth of who you are in all that you do.
And it can only be found by creating enough self-awareness to start choosing self-love over self-betrayal.

If you don't know where to begin, you can start by using the six tips I shared as a way to connect with the essence of your being and asking yourself: What drains me? What expands and inspires me? What do I daydream about? How can I bring more of who I am into my home? How can I build a stronger relationship with myself to hear and trust my intuition? And lastly, what do I need to believe in order to let go of the old me and invite in more of the real me?

DANEIKA GLENN

Daneika Glenn is an Artist, Blogger, Certified Wayfinder Life Coach, ICF Accredited Life Coach, author of the digital journaling course, The Woman You Were Always Meant To Be (learning2fly.org/product/digital-course), and the creator of Learning2fly.org and Learning2fly, LLC. She lives in Saint Paul, loves writing with Swarovski pens, swimming in the ocean, and engaging in soulful conversations.

She is on a mission to help women reconnect to their intuition, increase their confidence, and experience more joy by using their creativity to heal and empower their lives.

Check out her free five-day challenge: 5 Simple Practices To Navigate

Change (www.subscribepage.com/5-ways-to-say-goodbye-to-self-doubt) to start creating more of what you want.

Connect with Daneika at:
Website: learning2fly.org
Facebook: www.facebook.com/Learning2flycoach
Instagram: www.instagram.com/daneika_glenn
YouTube: www.youtube.com/@learning2flycoach/featured

BORN TO BREAK THE SHAME
I Choose Me!™

Darcey Kesner Hawkins

Did you tweet 'Me Too' in response to Actor Alyssa Milano's tweet in 2017?

It went viral around the globe almost instantly.

Within days of that tweet, Ms. Milano discovered that Tarana Burke, a community activist, had coined the phrase Me Too in 2006. Ms. Burke had built a movement for girls of color who suffered sexual assault (Britannica 2023).

These two powerful women came together to give a voice to victims by using the same phrase. Although a simple phrase, the meaning for the victims was profound. It represented two aspects of a crime committed against their gender by people who believed it was their right to inflict this type of violence; sexual assault within the workplace and childhood sexual assault.

On Facebook I wrote 'Me Too' and immediately deleted it. Even at 57 years old it was too much for me to share all of my truth.

But I was compelled to say something.

So, on October 18th, 2017, I posted "My heart breaks, prayers lifted for those who aren't ready to say… 'ME' too."

There; I felt complete.

In my mind I declared I was a victim by capitalizing the word me. Eventually, four people commented 'Me Too', then the commenting was over. I did nothing to encourage dialogue. What else could I say? I had buried this heinous act almost five decades prior. So, I didn't say anything. No one asked about it. In my mind, no one wanted to know about it anyway, so I did what I always do best.

I hid in plain sight once more.

Life's Ironies Were Lost on Me
Almost two years later, my book *Who is That in the Mirror?* was published. I had a burning need to help people figure out who they were outside of intergenerational trauma and how not to take half a century to get there.

I shared that my grandmother told me she took care of me because my parents neglected me. Sadly, my grandmother stretched the truth; my parents were focused on my sisters, my brother was an addict, and I felt invisible. And then, as an afterthought, I included in my book that

I was the victim of childhood sexual assault.

*****

My perfection skill set became razor sharp. I was adept at hiding and being that perfect child who matured into a perfect adult. The realization of what my book really represented, to me, was slow to sink in.

Writing it was a catalyst that turned my life upside down. Unlike Alice and her Wonderland at the bottom of her rabbit hole, the world I was dumped into wasn't a fantasy world, it was one of shame, denial, and pretense (Carroll 1893).

So dear reader, were you like me, in denial that you were affected by the abuse you experienced? Have you come to the point of accepting that it truly happened? This is a major distinction in your healing journey as it was in mine.

More Than Me Too

The Me Too movement was a very powerful shift in our collective consciousness; our shared beliefs, values, ideas, and knowledge that exists within our society. These survivors of abuse found the courage to share their stories and break the chains of silence. It has birthed a new paradigm of healing and self-empowerment.

However, in my healing journey, I lost touch with the Me Too movement. I know it paved the way for survivors to come forward, but it didn't have that impact for me. Possibly, it didn't for you either. When I dropped into my rabbit hole, I came to rest at the curve in the spiral of my 10th year of life, where a horrific act, The Event, was forced upon me. I was sexually abused by my step-grandfather.

> I was in shock and confused at the time.
> I was in denial then I buried it.
> It took five decades to rise to the surface.
> Fifty years of hiding and modifying my behavior for self-preservation.
> Even the Me Too movement didn't shake me out of my fear of sharing.

In 2020, the reception of the book I authored was a turning point. It was the readers' curiosity about The Event, surpassing my comfort level of sharing, that propelled me into my rabbit hole. I began to understand the enormity of what I casually shared. I had normalized my sexual trauma for too long and it was preventing me from healing.

Carrying the weight of these behaviors—normalizing trauma, denial of its existence, self-blame, and silence that binds us—is an immense burden to bear, hindering our ability to heal and find freedom.

The reality that abuse survivors live in doesn't follow a logical pattern that others understand; in many aspects it is easier for us to pretend it didn't happen. My belief was validated when I was admonished by a loved one for crying about the abuse. After reading my book he wanted to know why I wasn't angry at my abuser.

The simple answer was I hadn't journeyed to that point in my healing yet. The 10-year old girl still didn't understand what had happened.

This confrontation happened in 2020; I was still disassociated from The Event.

Logically, I understood the 10-year old girl was me. However, the traumatic event hadn't been addressed, let alone healed for my inner child; I was still awaiting integration as my adult self.

Now, unintentionally, more judgment was levied against me for not responding in an expected manner. It wasn't my loved one's fault for not understanding. It wasn't my fault for not understanding. Yet, regardless of fault, it was an additional level of "not enoughness" that I would have to heal through.

Hidden Disabilities
Dear reader, our healing journey resembles a roller coaster ride at times. We coax ourselves to the top of a rise with a multitude of healing methods only to plunge into depths of new, multi-faceted and deeply personal pain points.

It was a little over 20 years ago that major health organizations officially identified invisible disabilities. Twenty years is but a drop in the bucket when compared to the centuries trauma has existed. AND these disabilities are not invisible, they are hidden within the survivor, and the survivor experiences them every day, seven days a week, 365 days a year.

Hidden disabilities are not only created from sexual assault but any trauma including domestic violence, physical abuse, childhood neglect, combat and military trauma, accidents and catastrophic events, chronic illness, medical trauma, and probably more than this author is aware of at the time of writing. They can negatively affect our physical, emotional, and mental well-being. It is the hidden nature of these wounds that amplify the challenges we face, as the world may not have been educated yet on the depth of our struggles.

- Physically we may experience chronic pain or fatigue or other physical symptoms. These in turn affect our ability to engage in our lives, causing us frustration and to isolate. This is me. Can I directly tie my fibromyalgia to my trauma? No. However, it is one of the reasons I became a massage therapist.

  - We meet with doctors who find no physical corroborating evidence of our complaints. Some of us are labeled as malingerers and at worst, liars. Some of us are referred out to specialists who misdiagnose us and prescribe medication that exacerbate symptoms or create new conditions or diseases.

  - Some of us are fortunate and find doctors or naturopaths who are compassionate and understand.

  - Some of us give up and once again hide in plain sight. We try to assimilate, but we're always half a step off the rhythm of what we perceive as normal life.

- Emotionally we may be overwhelmed with feelings of anxiety, depression or PTSD. The impact of our trauma has left deep scars within us influencing our ability to trust and fully experience healthy relationships, including our relationship with ourselves, family, work, friends and even our capacity to engage in fulfilling sexual relationships; I am someone who has experienced this struggle with intimacy firsthand.

- We've learned to self-soothe with food, prescribed medications, illicit drugs or other products, binge watching our screens, or gambling. Some of us know we have addictive personalities, and we sincerely believe we are able to manage our behaviors without intervention.

- I parented my children while navigating my healing journey. I taught them to be fearful because I was afraid during their childhood. I protected them with fierceness, but I was helpless at the same time.

- The Universe led me to Emotional Freedom Technique (EFT) or tapping to ease my anxiety around many experiences in my life. I was astounded by the immediate benefits of the basic EFT course. Upon the offering of training as an EFT relationship coach, I enrolled and was certified in 2021 specializing in sex and intimacy. As always Creator gives alignment in my healing journey; tapping on my sexual assault was mandated in my training.

- Mentally we may have cognitive difficulties, memory loss, or difficulty concentrating. This negatively impacts our daily lives and also increases our frustration levels and further decreases our feelings of self-worth.

- We can adopt the attitude of 'fake it until we make it'. In psychology, there is evidence that this approach works. For me, my faking it was just that; a lie or my disordered brain would have had me believe so.

- I've adapted to my loss of certain long-term memories. I recognize that I must add strategies to assist in my learning retention. This is an on-going task.

I sincerely hope you don't identify with any of the examples I have shared with you thus far. However, I suspect you might as statistics from the RAINN website (Rape, Abuse & Incest National Network) show heartbreaking and sickening statistics (RAINN 2019). Acknowledging our behavior as trauma survivors, I have to ponder, what about the cases that are not reported? I know one individual who chose not to report two cases of rape, and at 10 years old in 1960 I certainly didn't report my assault.

Dear Reader, another distressing fact is the lack of discussion surrounding hidden disabilities which occurs with each and every assault and trauma.

I'm Shouting!
It is with my contribution to *Shout it From the Rooftops*, my resounding shout – **Born to Break the Shame** – that I call to dismantle the walls that have silenced survivors and perpetuated stigma surrounding trauma's hidden disabilities.

It was through the counsel of a wise woman and connection to the Universe that I channeled I was born to break the shame of what has hindered and tethered me to a false identity of conformity, to bring the conversation of trauma's hidden disabilities out in the open, and to provide a safe place for trauma survivors to gather and share our stories judgment free.

I Choose Me!™

Through the healing experiences that I have encountered over my lifetime, I have unequivocally declared, **I Choose Me!**™ It *"...is STARTING the first day of the REST of your LIFE…a life that prioritizes you first, that embraces and amplifies your gifts and intuition, and provides clarity in your purpose."* (Hawkins 2022)

The guidance of Spirit has not only directed me to explore, practice, and teach various healing methods such as shamanism, Reiki, massage therapy, EFT or tapping, and energy healing, but it has also instilled in me the realization that prioritizing self-care and self-love is paramount. This transformative journey, guided by spiritual influence and a developed intuition, has empowered me to honor and prioritize my own well-being, enabling me to better serve others on their spiritual and healing journeys. Becoming an ordained minister has been an additional calling that has further strengthened my connection to the spiritual realm and amplified my ability to support and guide others in their pursuit of spiritual growth and transformation.

*****

The Me Too movement has undeniably been an incredible start, empowering countless individuals to share their stories of abuse and break the silence that once held survivors captive. However, it's crucial to acknowledge that there's a population of people who require more support and healing; people like me and possibly you. This is where we should turn to the "I Choose Me!™" belief system. It harnesses the passion and determination of survivors, supplementing it with the next logical step towards healing and empowerment.

At its core, "I Choose Me!™" celebrates unity among survivors of trauma and abuse. It recognizes that the experiences of survivors are not isolated incidents but rather shared threads woven into the tapestry of our collective existence. By emphasizing the importance of supporting and standing with one another, the movement creates a space where we, the survivors, can find solace, understanding, and strength in our healing journeys.

It serves as a powerful reminder that we, the survivors, are not alone in our struggles, that our stories matter, and that our evolving healing is a vital part of the collective healing process. By coming together and breaking the cycle of silence and shame, we work hand in hand to help facilitate social change.

"I Choose Me!™" invites us to reclaim our power, prioritize our own well-being, and amplify our gifts. It recognizes that healing is not a linear process and that each individual's journey is unique. By embracing the idea of choosing oneself, we, the survivors, affirm our worthiness and create a pathway to personal transformation.

Infinite Healing

Where "I Choose Me!™" is the movement, Infinite Healing is the method and the heart of this movement. It transcends traditional ideas of healing. It recognizes that healing extends beyond temporary fixes or limited experiences, encompassing the multidimensional aspects of our being. It acknowledges that the effects of trauma and hidden disabilities modify our behaviors, often for decades or like myself, for half a century, and it calls us to break the cycle of shame and reclaim our authentic selves.

Embedded within "I Choose Me!™" is the profound concept of time travel within ourselves. The spiraling path of Infinite Healing takes us on a journey through the layers of our past, allowing us to heal old wounds, confront traumas, and transform pain into wisdom. Guided by our inner wisdom and aided by healing methods such as tapping, shamanic practices, coaching and ancestral knowledge, we courageously face our past and rewrite our narratives to reclaim fragments of our authentic selves.

As we spiral upward on our healing journey, we step into the present moment with a renewed sense of authenticity. We shed the masks of normalcy and societal expectations, embracing vulnerability and self-expression. In this state of alignment with our true selves, we radiate our unique essence to the world.

The spirals of healing continue into the present. They carry us as we weave new extensions to our tapestry, where we set the stage for the life we envision. With intention and conscious creation, we design our reality, manifesting our dreams and aspirations. We are the weavers of our destiny, intertwining our newfound authenticity into the fabric of our existence, crafting a vibrant tapestry of interconnectedness and purpose.

At the core of "I Choose Me!™" is the understanding that healing is an ongoing, infinite journey. It acknowledges that while challenges may arise, we have within us the power to heal, transform, and thrive; by ourselves or with our community. By prioritizing ourselves, embracing the "I Choose Me!™" mindset, and tapping into the infinite well of possibilities within us, we embark on a path of harmonious healing and self-realization.

So, if you are ready to take the next step on your healing journey, if you are ready to break the chains of shame and embrace your authentic self, the "I Choose Me!™" movement invites you to join. Together, we amplify our voices, support one another, and create a ripple effect of healing that extends far beyond our individual stories and time and into the tapestry of our community. I encourage you to embrace the power of Infinite Healing, choose yourself, and unlock the boundless possibilities that await you.

Poetry Medicine

One of the methods in which healing occurs is through self-expression, and one of the specific methods we use in Infinite Healing is called Poetry Medicine. Poetry Medicine is specifically designed as a sacred vessel to process emotions you may or may not realize you have caged within your body, safely daisy chain those emotions through one or several events, and express your emotions with this powerful experience of self-reflection.

Poetry Medicine in *Infinite Healing*
Ode to Soliloquy of Silence

by Darcey Kesner Hawkins

I was gifted the Soliloquy of Silence
when COVID visited me on Earth Day.
In literary terms, a soliloquy stops all action
so an actor may perform a monologue
to educate the audience to the unseen.

In that brilliant piece of writing
we are privy to what the character's motivations are.
But my gift lacked enlightenment
as the sound of silence descended
it was clear the gathering of knowledge was through my efforts alone.

The lack of busyness set the stage
for the presentation of my inner self's monologue
a sharing of truths I know nothing of.
I was immersed in an outpouring of angst, joy, fear, love and aha's
that soon filled over 40 pages and more of my journal.

I am being readied for my reveal.
The honor has been handed to me.
I balk at what this 3-D responsibility means.
"Why me?" I ask. "Why not you?" is the reply.
"What's so special about me?" "Nothing and everything."

I am both light and dark, as we all are.
I am thrust into this awareness.

to seek and maintain balance.
We must carve out the time for our Sacred Pause.
To take heed of our own Soliloquy.

References

Britannica, T. Editors of Encyclopaedia (2023, June 2). Tarana Burke. Encyclopedia Britannica. www.britannica.com/biography/Tarana-Burke

Carroll, L. (1893) Alice's Adventures in Wonderland. [New York, Boston, T. Y. Crowell & co] [Pdf] Retrieved from the Library of Congress, www.loc.gov/item/12031272/.

Hawkins, D. J. (2022, August 1). Rev. Darcey Kesner Hawkins. Retrieved July 20, 2023, from DarceyKesnerHawkins.com

RAINN. (2019) Scope of the Problem: Statistics. www.rainn.org/statistics/scope-problem

DARCEY KESNER HAWKINS

Darcey Kesner Hawkins can usually be found tussling for desk space with her black cat, Pi, who enjoys lying in front of the computer monitor and upon the keyboard. She is a passionate healer and a Spirit-led Modern Medicine Woman who knows the transformative power of self-healing firsthand. Having overcome childhood sexual assault, she now dedicates herself to serving and empowering others on their healing paths. As the founder of I Choose Me!™ Method & Movement, she leads the way in helping wounded individuals reclaim love in their lives, starting with themselves.

In her role as a Modern Medicine Woman, Darcey shares her expertise as a wellness intuitive & channeler, tapping into insights during massages and through touch. She also offers spiritual guidance and transformation as a minister and shamanic practitioner & healer. With certifications as a Reiki Master/Teacher and an EFT Relationship Coach, she ensures a holistic approach to healing.

Contact Information:
Website: www.DarceyKesnerHawkins.com
Email: info@DarceyKesnerHawkins.com
Facebook: www.facebook.com/Darcey.ModernMedicineWoman
Facebook: www.facebook.com/darcey.kesnerhawkins
Instagram: www.instagram.com/darcey_kesner_hawkins

PLEASURE AND VITALITY ARE YOUR BIRTHRIGHT
Redefining Womanhood on Your Own Terms

Falyn Morningstar

Societal Shackles

In the charming village of Liberty Road, a young girl named Falyn, just 7 years old, enjoyed a comfortable life with her caring family. They were in the process of constructing a beautiful two-story brick home on their expansive acre of land after moving to a nearby town with a reputedly better school district. Despite the love and care she received, Falyn often found herself overwhelmed with worry, fear, and a sense of lack that seemed to pervade her upbringing. This was unconscious at the time.

Whenever her parents had to leave, whether it was for a simple dinner, a weekend beach trip, or a camping adventure, Falyn would burst into tears. Each time they departed, she experienced an inexplicable feeling of abandonment, leaving her with a pervasive sense of insecurity. It was as though she could never feel entirely safe, and this emotion would resurface every time separation occurred.

Unfortunately, Falyn's family lacked the knowledge of healthy coping mechanisms, effective communication, and setting boundaries. Instead of encouraging her to express herself and process her emotions, they would brush off her tears with comments like, "You're a big girl now, don't cry." As a result, Falyn internalized the belief that showing emotions, particularly through tears, was inappropriate. She was denied the opportunity to properly mourn and be held in a space where her feelings could be validated and processed.

Society, in general, tends to stigmatize emotional expression and crying, chaining us to the notion that displaying vulnerability is a sign of weakness. This societal expectation forces many of us to suppress our emotions, shutting ourselves off from genuine expression and understanding.

It's essential to recognize that Falyn's upbringing and her family's response were not deliberate acts of harm but rather reflections of the cultural norms they were embedded in. By acknowledging the importance of emotional expression and learning healthy coping strategies, individuals and communities can break free from the shackles of these misconceptions and create a more supportive environment for emotional growth and healing.

The repercussions of an ostensibly innocent yet inappropriate experience of pleasure exploration between children can be profound. For Falyn, who was just 7 years old at the time, this encounter left a lasting impact on her nervous system, leading her to develop a deep-seated mistrust. In her young mind, life was an unsafe space that did not prioritize her well-being.

Unfortunately, her parents were not present to shield her from this experience, and the absence of their protection has had lasting consequences on her life and romantic relationships to this day. The wounds from this early encounter have shaped her perceptions and interactions, making it challenging for her to form healthy and trusting connections with others, especially in romantic contexts.

Falyn was raised to believe that her role as a woman was to be modest, unassuming, and self-sacrificing – a pattern she observed in the women around her. The notion of abandoning oneself to serve others and seeking love externally became ingrained in her, and she followed suit.

Growing up, Falyn's modest upbringing stifled any exploration or discussion about her own body, including her sexuality. Pleasure was considered a taboo topic and remained unaddressed. While sex education in health class existed, there was a glaring absence of information about the female anatomy, particularly the clitoris, which houses over 5000 nerve endings and is a key pleasure center for women. It wasn't until her late 20s that Falyn learned about this crucial aspect of her body. This societal limitation continues to hinder women from fully embracing and experiencing their innate radiance and potential.

Falyn's journey into "womanhood" began at 13 with her first period. Despite experiencing several yeast infections between ages 13 and 18, the doctors offered only temporary fixes like pills or washes, neglecting to address potential dietary factors. Reflecting on it now, the lack of awareness back then is frustrating.

At just 14, Falyn endured an excruciating bladder infection that caused her screams of pain to echo through the hospital waiting room, leaving emotional scars and further disconnecting her from her sense of power.

Throughout her teenage years, Falyn relied on toxic tampons and started taking the birth control pill at 16 to prevent pregnancy. She continued using it until she reached 26. Some reflections:

- Every time a tampon is inserted, it scrapes the delicate lining inside the vagina, obstructing the natural, healthy flow of blood that plays a crucial role in purifying a woman's body.

- In reality, women are fertile for only about 6-7 days each month, yet society heavily promotes the use of contraceptive pills during the most critical stages of reproductive development.

- Unfortunately, women are often not adequately informed about the detrimental effects of taking contraceptive pills. Let's explore a few of these impacts:
    - Mineral deficiencies, such as magnesium, vitamin A, and B-vitamins, can push their bodies into a state of survival mode (sympathetic), adversely affecting their adrenals and thyroid.
    - The ingestion of fortified iron (in the pill) can lead to oxidative damage, particularly in the organs,

exacerbating health issues.

- Synthetic estrogen, a component of many contraceptive pills, can disrupt metabolism, contributing to insulin resistance and hormonal imbalances like estrogen dominance.

- Astonishingly, the pill can disconnect a woman's pleasure center and brain, interfering with the intimate connection between physical pleasure and emotional well-being.

- Moreover, being on the pill may affect a woman's outlook on partner selection, creating a sort of blinders effect that hinders them from choosing partners who truly deserve their time and trust. Falyn's experience with partner selection reflected the sense of unworthiness and confusion that can arise while on the pill, causing her to distrust her own intuition.

It is vital to raise awareness about these consequences and to empower women with knowledge that allows them to make informed choices about their reproductive health. Encouraging open discussions and providing accurate information about alternative contraceptive options can help women make decisions that align with their overall well-being and personal values.

The rest of high school seemed like a blur, and college became an escape to have some fun and numb the unconscious pain. However, shortly after turning 21, Falyn found herself in trouble with the police. This incident acted as a wake-up call, tempering her wildness and leading to fewer nights of getting blacked out. Despite these external changes, Falyn remained disconnected from her body, unable to fully feel her emotions or listen to her heart. Like much of society, she had never been taught proper coping skills or the importance of checking in with oneself.

After graduating alongside her sorority sisters, Falyn began her big girl job in local government, back in her hometown. Little did she know that this seemingly ordinary step would mark the beginning of a journey that would be both traumatic and liberating.

The Mentor

Many of us lack the privilege of encountering wise mentors who can support and strengthen us as we navigate life. Creating a safe space for others to be themselves is a skill that eludes many, as they themselves struggle to be grounded within their own being.

Falyn, from a very young age, experienced events that made her feel unsafe, leaving a lasting imprint on her nervous system. This belief that people close to her were not safe and that life itself was unsafe shaped her choices in partners, gravitating towards those who were familiar but not necessarily good for her well-being. Sometimes, the allure of familiarity can overshadow the potential for growth and transformation.

At the age of 22-23, Falyn endured heartbreak from a disloyal man, causing immense pain and shame. To cope with these emotions, she built a shield of armor with her physical body, immersing herself in powerlifting and bodybuilding training. While this outlet helped her on a physical level, her emotional body remained unconscious during this time. Falyn's focus on achievement and constant motion became her measure of worthiness.

In the midst of this journey, Falyn encountered a life-changing mentor at a private family-knit gym. This mentor served as a male friend who supported her through dark times, providing encouragement and showing her the true meaning of friendship. His unwavering support and presence were instrumental in her growth and healing.

Over the next three years, Falyn delved deep into powerlifting and bodybuilding training, finding solace and strength in the gym. During this period, she abstained from sexual activity, even with herself, as her mental focus was on relentless achievement and pushing forward.

Throughout her journey of self-discovery, the Universe blessed Falyn with numerous mentors, each over a decade older than her. These mentors offered her love, wisdom, and encouragement, guiding her as she navigated the complexities of life and her inner world. Their influence played a pivotal role in shaping her perspective and allowing her to embrace her true self.

The power of mentorship cannot be overstated, especially when it comes from individuals with a wealth of life experience. These mentors provided Falyn with the support and guidance she needed to break free from past traumas and emerge into a more empowered and authentic version of herself. Their nurturing presence inspired her to pursue her passion for health and wellness, becoming a beacon of inspiration for others on their own journey of self-discovery.

The Opposition and Awakening Start

Every woman has experienced some form of rupture in her life, whether it be sexual abuse, emotional violation, or neglect. These painful experiences shatter our trust and dim our radiance, affecting both us and the world around us.

The suppression of our radiance often leads to anger. We navigate through life with our light turned off, a protective mechanism from past traumas. It's important to acknowledge that this self-preservation served us well at the time.

Unfortunately, generational trauma and societal conditioning often leave women doubting their intuition and innate wisdom. Falyn's own journey of self-discovery involved focusing on improving her physical body through weightlifting while juggling a full-time job in local government and part-time grad school. She even acquired a personal training certification to pursue her passion for fitness. However, she believed she had to follow a conventional career path to gain approval from her family.

Years of this fast-paced, demanding lifestyle eventually took a toll on her health, manifesting in various symptoms:
- Abnormal hair loss
- Body odor
- Severe fatigue
- Delayed muscle soreness after workouts

- Bloating
- Emotional eating
- Insomnia with a constant wired and tired feeling
- Clotting during her withdraw bleed when taking birth control pills, which she eventually stopped, leading to further symptoms and the disappearance of her period for several months.

Unfortunately, traditional doctors couldn't provide answers or solutions, leaving Falyn frustrated. However, she discovered functional lab testing through a friend's experience, and it turned out to be the key to starting her healing journey.

Through food sensitivity, hormone, and stool testing, Falyn finally found validation for her symptoms. Armed with a roadmap for healing, she made significant changes to her lifestyle and incorporated natural supplements to restore balance.

The knowledge she gained about integrative and holistic living was life-changing for Falyn, and she knew she wanted to become a practitioner to help others. Prioritizing the welfare of the mind, body, and soul became the core of her approach, addressing every cell, tissue, and organ.

After being a client for about 6-8 months, Falyn decided to take the year-long certification program through Functional Diagnostic Nutrition (FDN) to become a practitioner herself. This was her way of transforming her long-standing passion for health and wellness, which had always been in the background, into a fulfilling and impactful profession.

Falyn's journey showcases the power of self-awareness, self-care, and the importance of embracing unconventional approaches to well-being. By reclaiming her radiance and pursuing her true passion, she empowers herself and others to live vibrant and fulfilled lives.

Breaking the Chains

Falyn embraced the challenging path of redefining womanhood and liberating herself from oppressive chains that had burdened her at just 26 years old. She believes in the principle of reaping what one sows, knowing that her efforts to break free from societal expectations would yield profound rewards.

To empower herself further, Falyn delved into various pillars of self-improvement taught by FDN (Functional Diagnostic Nutrition). Addressing her diet, rest, exercise, stress reduction, and supplementation became essential components of her transformative journey.

However, despite these positive changes, something still felt amiss. It was during this time that she was introduced to a quantum voyance integration coach based in Hawaii. Working with this practitioner for three months, Falyn experienced astonishing breakthroughs. In a powerful vision, she saw her strong physical body carrying the almost withered, skeletal form of her emotional body. This stark image was an eye-opening revelation. Remarkably, after the three months, the vision returned, but this time with a transformative twist. Her physical, emotional, and even spiritual bodies were seated together, arm in arm, overlooking a majestic mountainous view. The once weak and vulnerable emotional body now started to radiated vitality with muscle and skin.

Embracing the journey of self-discovery, Falyn sought further support over the next four years. She engaged in therapies such as eye movement desensitization and reprocessing (EMDR), talk therapy, internal family systems (parts work), and somatic experiencing. Each therapy brought her greater awareness of her true self. Beyond therapy, she immersed herself in books that explored the intricacies of the physical, emotional, and spiritual aspects of being human. Daily meditation practice became an integral part of her healing journey.

With an ever-deepening understanding of herself, Falyn realized it was time to break free from the corporate life chains that continued to impinge on her well-being. Working in the life and health insurance industry (which came after the local government job), she came to a pivotal realization – she yearned to be on the other side, supporting individuals' healing journeys instead of merely offering pills or prescription drug plans. She wanted to genuinely help people get better and facilitate their well-being. This newfound sense of purpose and calling drove her towards a path of greater fulfillment and service.

Challenges and Triumphs
In our inherent power and sacredness lies the treasure we seek. Finding it requires staying curious and being our own health advocate. Falyn's journey exemplifies the challenges and triumphs of embracing this path.
One challenge Falyn faced after seemingly healing her initial symptoms (noted above). During a standard blood test called a CBC, she

discovered a high iron level, which she attributed to taking Brewer's Yeast, a recommendation from a previous coach. Additionally, Falyn carried one SNP for hemochromatosis, a condition where the body can naturally absorb too much iron. This revelation shed light on her grandmother's history of receiving iron injections during pregnancy, potentially contributing to the iron overload. The accumulation of iron in her tissues led to distress in her liver, pancreas, and gallbladder. Falyn wondered if this iron overload could be responsible for her chronic fatigue, digestive issues, and hormone imbalances. Considering that fortified iron is present in various foods she had consumed since childhood, and the birth control pill also contained it, Falyn recognized the significant impact of this excess iron, which could not simply dissipate but became stuck in her body.

However, Falyn triumphed over these challenges when the Universe guided her to the Root Cause Protocol, founded by Morley Robbins. Over the course of 1-1.5 years, she diligently followed the protocol, donating blood three times to excrete the excess iron and remove it from her tissues. She also underwent several Full Monty tests and a Hair Tissue Mineral Analysis to identify any mineral deficiencies and metal overloads. This thorough analysis led her to a surprising discovery - high uranium levels, which indicated the presence of high radon in her home. Armed with this knowledge, she took steps to address the issue, potentially saving herself and her family from the risks of cancer caused by this silent but deadly threat.

Another challenge Falyn confronted was related to her thyroid. Experiencing tightness in her throat on and off, along with fatigue and a slowed metabolism, Falyn wondered about the correlation between her throat chakra (Vishuddha) and her thyroid gland in the spiritual sense. The throat chakra is associated with communication, expression, and authenticity, and Falyn's struggles with her throat and metabolism prompted a realization. She observed that many women with thyroid issues often struggle with speaking their truth and adhering to societal expectations of womanhood. The interconnectedness between the throat chakra and the womb space intrigued her. As she learned to express her truth, it seemed to align with the healing of her womb, creating a harmonious connection between the vocal cords and pelvic floor, as well as the throat and cervix. Understanding this link encouraged Falyn to explore the connection and expression of her pleasure center and vocal cords, as she wondered what her body was trying to convey.

Throughout her journey, Falyn emphasizes the importance of somatic awareness and being present in our bodies. She recognizes that as children, our awareness is primarily focused on bodily sensations, but as we grow older, external interactions may cause us to lose touch with our innate capacity for awareness. However, somatic tools can facilitate healing from trauma and attachment wounds. By directing awareness towards feelings and behaviors that create blocks and dissociation, we can understand the origins of protective parts within us. Acknowledging and appreciating these parts for their important work can lead to the emergence of vulnerable parts, strengthening our self-understanding and growth.

Falyn firmly believes that our body possesses its own innate awareness, engaging in communication and connection within itself, making it a powerful resource for healing and self-discovery. By reconnecting with this inner awareness, we open ourselves up to profound transformation and a deeper understanding of our embodied selves.

Continued Integration of Love

Falyn understands that your anger is valid and that it's okay to feel tightness in your throat and chest. Emotions are a result of past experiences, especially those with intense emotional reactions that create long-term memories. Recognizing this, you can learn to transform pain and suffering into joy and inspiration.

Dr. Joe Dispenza's revelation that people spend 70% of their lives in survival mode resonated deeply with Falyn. Looking back on her own life, she realized she had been trying to survive, please others, and seek external validation.

The journey of self-discovery involves falling apart to come back together. Falyn is learning to accept her different parts, understanding that they all have good intentions and deserve to be heard.

As women, we are beyond measure. Our essence extends beyond pleasure alone; it's an opportunity for sisterhood and mutual support. By embracing all parts of ourselves, we can recreate a world where women's voices and bodies are valued and celebrated.

This path isn't without challenges, but through presence, acknowledgement, and integration, Falyn inspires others to harmonize their physical, mental/emotional, and spiritual selves.
She emphasizes the importance of not trading pieces of yourself away or seeking validation externally. Instead, coming into inner union and

reclaiming your power unleashes the most potent force of transformation.

Falyn continues on this journey, encouraging others to do the same and reclaim their inner power. By embracing your wholeness, you can be enraptured by the pleasures of life. Let your magnetism shine and be a force of positive change in the world.

The New Era

Being a woman is an offering, a masterpiece, and your presence itself is a sacred ceremony.

In a world where external validation often dictates our sense of worth, let this message be a reminder that worthiness is not something to be earned or bestowed upon you; it is an intrinsic aspect of your being, independent of achievements, possessions, or losses. Love and acceptance are woven into the very fabric of who you are. Your worth resides in your heart, a precious gift awaiting acknowledgment. Embrace the truth that you deserve love and acceptance just as you are. Pleasure is no longer taboo; it is a natural aspect of human existence. Women who once felt confined by societal expectations now stand tall, proud of their identities and their right to pleasure. *Reflect on experiences that have disconnected you from yourself.*

Release the need for validation from others and recognize that your worth always resides within you, even during uncertain times. Know that you are enough and deserving of love and abundance. Embrace your intrinsic worth with every breath, radiating self-acceptance and love into the world. You possess the power to claim your worth and walk confidently in the light of your own value. Women who distrust this intuitive knowing diminish their power, leading to physical and emotional concerns. *Consider how disconnection from self has affected your well-being.*

The world is evolving into a place where women celebrate their bodies, voices, emotions, and desires without reservation. Freed from outdated norms, women embrace the essence of femininity and claim their birthright to pleasure and vitality with open hearts. *Reflect on your deepest desires and aspirations. How can you reconnect with your radiance?*

Let's raise our voices, sisters, and proclaim, "Vitality and Pleasure Are My Birthright!" We redefine womanhood on our own terms.

FALYN MORNINGSTAR

Through personal challenges and a lack of support from traditional western practitioners, Falyn struggled with various health concerns like digestive discomfort, insomnia, fatigue, hair loss, muscle soreness, an irregular cycle, and emotional eating. However, her journey led her to discover the transformative power of eastern modalities. Delving into Functional Diagnostic Nutrition, she gained profound insights that inspired her to become a certified Practitioner herself. Delving further into her well-being, Falyn found support and addressed difficulties related to sexual and childhood trauma, attachment, anxiety, iron dysregulation, and thyroid imbalances. Having experienced the frustration and loneliness of feeling like something was always missing, she now guides curious and driven health-minded women on a similar journey toward wholeness and vibrance. Her approach is integrative and holistic, using functional lab testing, sonic healing, and somatic tools to help women reconnect with their inner power, vitality, and pleasure. Falyn embraces the motto "Heal Together, Rise Together."

Email: discover@falynmorningstar.com
Instagram: www.instagram.com/falynmorningstar
Facebook: www.facebook.com/falyn.morningstar
LinkedIn: www.linkedin.com/in/falyn-morningstar
Free discovery call: calendly.com/power-fal

Vitality & Pleasure Meditation just for you:

EMBRACE YOURSELF! BE KIND TO YOURSELF!
Your shadows that follow you will become lighter!

Muhnoo Sophia Jain

Lean into your shadow and you will see the depths of your past disappear. As you pave a new path the shadows will become clear…

A little while ago, I visited the beach with my dear friend Hollis and my daughter. The sun gleamed, the sand glistened, and the salty air filled our hearts. I took a picture of our shadows- the stillness was captivating. I was reminded of how our shadow follows us no matter where we go.

This visual recently led me to understand our shadow from a more profound level – something I wish to pass on as a legacy to you. Sometimes in our formative years, we can experience a situation where a parent, a loved one, or someone close to us is often consumed in their own lives neglecting and failing to meet our emotional needs. In a world where we are meant to feel safe, their actions can leave us feeling incomplete, hurt, and dismissed. As we grow into adults prior to healing, we can become accustomed to seeking external validation.

These experiences then serve as the ghosts of our pasts following us like shadows no matter where we try to go.

In order to truly enjoy the moment and the experience we are living through, we have to transcend through the ghosts of our past 'not just merely let go' from our minds. We have to understand and appreciate the reason for the pain before redefining it. Only then can we truly let it go! This has to be discovered and embraced in our own unique ways.

To what lengths are you willing to go to heal yourself? Do you have enough support? Are you keeping yourself safe? When you come face to face with the demons of your past, you won't always have a game plan- but as long as you remain true to yourself, the parts revealed will continue to transform and transmute safely and lovingly. At each moment, show yourself the same compassion and kindness you would a lost child.

Anger turned inward is sadness. It is vital to allow yourself to acknowledge this anger and express it in healthy ways before it starts to haunt you and follow you everywhere you go. We must be courageous and embrace that we deserve to feel whole and complete.

I had to heal my soul before I could find my soulmate— Become attuned with my own emotions and come face to face with people who have hurt me. I learned to interact genuinely by meeting them where they were. If that was not possible, I had to let go of any expectations from them. This was liberating! As Linda Ugelow would say, "it is the act of practicing forgiverance where forgiving delivers us and sets us free."

Once we become present with what we are experiencing, we learn to remain true to our inner self even if our conscious mind overcomes and compensates through logic and reasoning. With practice, we can master this!

"As daunting as leaning into your shadow can be, every day is a new opportunity to grow. Everybody has a past that affects them, but it can affect you a lot less if you work to improve yourself." –George Murdock

MUHNOO SOPHIA JAIN

Muhnoo Sophia Jain was born in India and moved to New Jersey at sixteen. Muhnoo's early work was published in the "Teen Scene" in the Star Ledger, "Excelsior" Rutgers Preparatory School Magazine, "Mosaic Literary Magazine" at Rutgers University, among others. She received the Outstanding Achievements in Poetry by the International Society of Poets in 2003. Muhnoo created and supported the "Because I Belong project" which served underprivileged youth. Muhnoo is a visionary who is committed to her life's purpose of empowering others to recognize their value. Muhnoo is a therapist and provides mental health support for families and individuals. Muhnoo resides with her daughter Siyona, a budding writer who authored *The Dog Shelter* and supports the Animal Welfare

Association (available on Amazon):

The Dog Shelter on Amazon: htttps://a.co/d/7oH0jr2
LinkedIn: linkedin.com/in/manu-sophia-jain-kumar-282b8183
Instagram: www.instagram.com/muhnoosophia
Facebook: www.facebook.com/manu.k.33

SHOWING UP MESSY
Because That's Who I Am Today

Suzy Roundy-Schmidt

Sweet, sweet surrender
Live, Live without care
Like a fish in the water
Like a bird in the air
– John Denver

The plan was that each morning I would wake up and live intentionally through the day. Striving to be mindful and present in every moment, and to be my authentic self. Living without care – like a fish in the water, like a bird in the air. This was the plan and the plan never worked. I used to shame myself for having big emotions during the day or going the other way and not engaging with the world. I even started to question who my own authentic self was. It was then that I began to realize, I was not the problem – *the plan was the problem.*

Why? Because I am a messy, complicated human and like all messy, complicated humans, I have feelings, I make plans and they don't always work out, and things around me aren't stagnant - they are always changing. And it is up to me to either go with the flow or react to these things. There is a best version of myself that I always wanted people to see, so I would hide the things that I found unattractive. The result? I didn't like myself very much. By pushing down, hiding and denying these parts, I began to hate these parts of myself. That's when I decided to make a new plan.

I decided to acknowledge these parts of myself; to make friends with them and see what it was that they needed, and I found out some pretty amazing things. Those parts that I had been running away from were usually connected to the biggest learning experiences of my life. The things that I tried and failed. The times when I was not showing up as the person I really wanted to be. I also realized that some of the things I was pushing down were not even real! They were things that other people had made me believe. I never would have found these things out, if I had continued to ignore and hide them.

I wonder, as a fellow human, what are the things that you are
- Pushing down
- Denying
- Hating

about yourself?

I am offering you my experience and my hand to help you start to walk down a new path. The one to your truly authentic self – the "good" and the "bad." Did you know that we don't even have to label our experiences? We can just acknowledge them and look at lessons learned.

Are you ready to start your journey to embrace ALL of you and be ready to live your life out loud? It will feel so freeing that you will want to shout it from the rooftops!!

You've gotta get up and try, try, try –Pink

I know, easier said than done. Did you know that you don't have to tackle everything all at once? You can do just a little bit at a time. Feel it out a little bit. I like to think of it as an investigation – how would you approach it if you were a detective? Take some time to stand back and take in the big picture. Then, I encourage you to think about one of those places that you feel shame. Don't jump into the shame, just notice it – where is it sitting? What does it look like? Is it solid? Does it move? Just observe. Maybe say hello and let that part know that you are here to understand and to help it understand. Does this part have anything that it wants to tell you? Does it know why shame is there?

Some questions to maybe discuss:
- Is this yours to hold onto? Whatever the uncomfortable feeling, whatever the thoughts are that are attached to this. Is it really yours? Or
- Is it something that someone else has put there?
- Did someone else make you think that you had flaws?
- Who made you feel that you weren't or aren't good enough?

I am here to tell you that WE get to decide. Not somebody else.
Life is definitely hard and sometimes we do things to protect ourselves that we might not be proud of. We might not even recognize our

reasoning behind what we do, and it is important to understand. For instance, I can become very closed off from people very quickly. I always saw this quality as "flaky" for not being able to keep relationships and connections, I held an expectation I should be able to maintain these relationships and connections. Once I made friends with this part of myself, it reminded me we have been hurt, throughout our life, by many people. And, it was usually by people we were close to. This helped me to realize that when I started to get "too close" to people, I would slam on the brakes to avoid being hurt – even though this strategy really didn't work. I was hurting myself by letting go of positive relationships. Now, I can recognize this all too familiar pattern when it starts to play out and instead of making the scared, protective part handle it alone, I can bring in my older, wiser self and we can make decisions that work for both of us.

Hello darkness, my old friend. I've come to talk with you again.
–Simon & Garfunkel

I don't want to give you the idea that investigating, understanding, and befriending these pieces will be easy. I definitely still have days when I revert back to not liking these parts. When old, negative patterns start to pop up, I get annoyed, frustrated and sad. Sometimes, I just want to get back into bed and not deal with any of it, and that is okay. What I know now is all I can do is my best at that moment. And feelings move and they shift and I will not feel this way forever. And, this is a perfect time to show myself compassion. This can include doing something nice for myself, reaching out to others, journaling, maybe even just taking a shower. Reminding myself I don't always have to be "on." The most important thing to do is remember to let this move through you

– don't try to stop it, you don't want to get stuck in that place. You can come out on the other side. Winston Churchill once said, "If you are going through hell, keep going."

I also encourage you to remember just because something is uncomfortable, it doesn't mean it is bad.

> *I need your grace*
> *To remind me*
> *To find my own*
> *—Snow Patrol*

The truth is, we can't do these things alone. As humans, we are social beings. We are hardwired to connect. Imagine, back in the day, living in a small village where you have to depend on others to live. It was not a wise choice to stand out, to be different. Anyone who disrupted the status quo would likely be a problem. Imagine Salem, Massachusetts circa 1692. The truth is, witches were accused, tried, and hanged – both women and men. Toeing the line has been deeply conditioned into us to the point our body reacts with worry and fear if we step over that line.

That being said, we now live in a society where we can find others who are like us – and yes, sometimes they are hard to find and it may be exhausting to look, AND it will totally be worth it. It is time to reclaim your space – push the boundaries and live to make your soul happy. You can let go of things that no longer serve you whether it is an idea, thought, or behavior. You can learn to love your entire self because who you are today is a compilation of all of those parts.

They can kick dirt in your face
Dress you down, and tell you that your place
Is in the middle, when they hate the way you shine
—Brandi Carlisle

I see you, I hear you, I am you.

Just know you are not alone. Every day is a different adventure. Some will be good, some not so much, but just know that doing the best you can, in that moment is all you need to do. And you get to decide what that looks like.

You are enough. Right here, right now. No matter what.

Pretty, pretty please, don't you ever, ever feel
Like you're less than fuckin' perfect
Pretty, pretty please, if you ever, ever feel like you're nothing
You're fuckin' perfect to me
—Pink

SUZY ROUNDY-SCHMIDT

Suzy Roundy-Schmidt is a compassionate psychotherapist who uses her warmth, humor, and deep understanding of human nature to help others. She loves to spend her free time in nature, walking in the woods. Suzy is also an avid music lover, recognizing music has been the only real constant in her life. She also has a real soft spot for animals, and as a chicken mom, Suzy has found solace in watching her feathered family members stroll around her backyard while she relaxes in the sunshine, with her two Boston Terriers. Not one to take life too seriously, Suzy is always up for a good laugh and prides herself on being able to make others smile through her funny anecdotes and witty humor.

Facebook: www.facebook.com/suzy.roundyschmidt.5
Instagram: www.instagram.com/being_suzyrs
TikTok: www.tiktok.com/@being_suzyrs
Website: www.suzyrs.com

Shout It From The Rooftops Playlist

PEOPLE CAN CHANGE
Even When You Least Expect It

Trisha Singeltary

Dad started using cocaine when I was young. It was a common party drug in the 80's. It started off as a fun way to let loose, like having a gin and tonic after work. By the late 80's it was a real problem, he was addicted. On the outside, Dad was charming and successful, working in the entertainment business, a pioneer for a black man of that time. On the inside, in his personal life, he was a mess. There was excessive gambling, prostitutes, and who knows what else. I don't know why I thought in all this he would also be able to be my Dad. He wasn't capable. I'd invite him to school events, which he would insist he would come to, like the time I sang in a small ensemble group. He never showed up. Dad was there for big events like graduations and paid for needed items like new shoes. I chased Dad for years, a glutton for rejection and not fully understanding addiction. After college I decided," that's it, I give up! I'm not chasing him anymore!" I needed to let go of the father I wanted in order to accept the one I had. There was peace in this decision. It was good timing because at the same time Dad moved on to crack.

Like people say, "crack is whack". It was a nightmare. He was having delusions, extreme paranoia, and was angry. The charm and the sense of humor he had vanished. These were dark times. I kept my distance. I didn't know how to help, none of us did. We had several interventions with him and he had been in several expensive intensive treatment centers. I thought, we have lost him forever. Well, it's hard to lose someone you never had.

One day when I was an adult, just like that, snap, Dad quit drugs. I didn't want to believe it and get my hopes up. I had been there before. Dad would come out of one of his expensive treatment centers talking about how he was ready, only to go right back to them weeks later. Suddenly the Dad I had chased for years started reaching out to me, wanting to meet for lunch. I wondered how long the new Dad would last. He's been clean for about fifteen years. I am so glad he is not hurting himself anymore. Dad takes antidepressants regularly, which keeps him level but are not a perfect fix. He was there for me at a very crucial time, when my mom was diagnosed with cancer. None of my family came through like Dad. Some called and sent text messages. My friends showed up, which helped me get through some of the most difficult days of my life. It was during Covid. He stepped up in a big way and I will never forget it. The day of mom's memorial, a couple hours before, Dad calls to tell me he will not attend. This hurt deeply, Cocaine Dad resurfaced and the little girl in me felt abandoned again. Dad could never handle certain things, drugs or not. That one action could never remove all the good. He did the best he knew how to do.

Now Dad dances at family parties, playing some of our favorite songs. He enjoys his grandkids and makes sure he shows up for them in ways he couldn't for his kids. Can people change? Yes, now I know that it is possible. Maybe not overnight and not under the same circumstances. Each person is so different. If someone really wants to change and is prepared to do the work necessary for this to happen, I believe they can.

TRISHA SINGELTARY

Trisha Singletary has had the joy of teaching art for twenty six years in New York and Los Angeles. She studied Illustration at Parsons School of Design in New York, receiving a Bachelors of Art and then went on to a Masters of Fine Art from New York University. While teaching art, she has shown her art in galleries, created art for commission, and worked on some freelance projects.

Currently, Trisha is working on artwork influenced by her 23 & Me findings, exploring African textiles and patterns in conjunction with paintings.. She looks forward to sharing this work with the public in the coming year. In her free time, Trisha enjoys playing with her cat, gardening, salsa dancing, journaling, and spending time with friends.

Email: tsingletary@wesleyschool.org
Instagram: www.instagram.com/singletaryart22

I AM CREATIVE PUBLISHING

"Creativity goes beyond a pencil and a paintbrush." – Hollis Citron

Hello everyone, my name is Hollis Citron. I am so happy that you are in this space reading and benefiting from the wisdom of these incredible humans!

A little about me. I have been an art educator for 30 years and have worked with so many people of all different ages, abilities and backgrounds. It has been such a gift. It has really brought to light a passion and constant reminder to me to be an active listener and observer to then be guided for others to have permission to explore possibilities and feel expressive.

I Am Creative has been created to enhance the power and awareness of the written word. Pepple are willing to be vulnerable and they write and share experiences and perspectives, which is such a gift to both the writer and reader and it feels so expansive. I believe that by people sharing their stories, which as we know is an ancient tradition, it binds us together and creates stronger connections on both a physical, psychological and spiritual level. There is such power in the written word.

The mission here is to shine the spotlight for each individual, both authors and readers, to feel expressive and empowered.

We each have stories that shape us but do not have to define us.
We are works in progress. I truly believe and have seen it over and over again that when a person sees themselves as a creator they feel purposeful and are at their core happier individuals.

I Am Creative is all about creating that safe space for all to have permission to let your guard down and allow you to explore YOU and quiet that inner voice in your head that may not be so supportive at times, do you know that voice?

Please bring this as a mantra into your life so you can get it into your subconscious and don't let anyone else tell you otherwise…

"I Am Creative… I Am Expressive… I Am Worthy."

Hollis Citron is the Founder & CEO of I Am Creative and I Am Creative Publishing. Check out my podcast, I Am Creative with Hollis

Citron, that is all about expanding the definition of creativity beyond a pencil and a paintbrush.

Website: www.iamcreativephilly.com
Facebook: www.facebook.com/iamcreativephilly
Podcast: creativeconversations.podbean.com.
Instagram: www.instagram.com/iamcreativephilly
Publishing: www.iamcreativephilly.com/express-yourself-publishing-house

Check out the I Am Creative Publishing website:

www.ingramcontent.com/pod-product-compliance
Lightning Source LLC
Chambersburg PA
CBHW051650040426
42446CB00009B/1072